Once Upon a Time...

STORY·SERMONS FOR·CHILDREN

John Timmer

ZondervanPublishingHouse
Academic and Professional Books
Grand Rapids, Michigan

A Division of HarperCollinsPublishers

ONCE UPON A TIME: Story Sermons for Children
Copyright © 1992 by John Timmer

Requests for information should be addressed to:
Zondervan Publishing House
Academic and Professional Books
Grand Rapids, Michigan 49530

Library of Congress Cataloging-in-Publication Data

Timmer, John, 1927–
    Once upon a time: story sermons for children / John Timmer.
        p.   cm.
    Summary: A collection of stories reflecting the many facets of God's world.
    ISBN 0-310-58621-6
    1. Children's sermons. [1. Sermons. 2. Christian life.] I. Title.
BV4315.T55   1992   92-5658
252'.53—dc20   CIP
                                                                          AC

Edited by Robert D. Wood
Cover design by Gary Gnidovic

Printed in the United States of America

92 93 94 95 96 97 / ML / 10 9 8 7 6 5 4 3 2 1

To the children at Woodlawn

Contents

SPECIAL-DAY STORIES

Stories for Advent and Christmas

Stories for Holy Week and Easter

Stories for the Season of Pentecost

A Story for the Celebration of the Lord's Supper

Introduction

Once Upon a Time is a collection of stories for children. They can be read by parents to their children, or they can be told by teachers to their students in a church school or Christian school setting. Or they can be used by pastors as children's sermons.

These stories are not object lessons. Nor are they moralistic tales. Rather, they reflect the outlandishness of grace and the topsy-turviness of the kingdom of God.

Once Upon a Time is a collection of stories I have used over many years in my parish ministry. They tell in simple story language the same message I have been preaching from the pulpit.

Many of the stories are my own. Most of them I have garnered from a wide variety of sources. As much as possible, I have given credit, but in a few cases I am unable to trace the source. I apologize to the parents of these orphans.

I am indebted to a number of people for bringing stories to my attention. I am especially indebted to my secretary, Mary Brasser, for her assistance in bringing my language down to the level of small children.

1

Why the Sky Is Blue

Do you children know this song:

> *Tell me why the stars do shine;*
> *Tell me why the ivy twines;*
> *Tell me why the sky's so blue;*
> *And I will tell you just why I love you.*

Last week, when the weather was so beautiful and there wasn't a cloud in the sky, this song popped into my head. Suddenly I found myself singing, "Tell me why the sky's so blue."

Then I thought: Maybe this is why. Maybe, when God was creating the world, he looked down from heaven and said, "Something is still missing. Some color. Yes, that's it. What the seas and the oceans need is some color."

So God quickly created the angels and told them, "Do you see all that blue paint over there? Each of you grab a can and a brush and go down and paint the seas and the oceans."

Quickly the angels did what God told them. They each grabbed a can of paint and a brush, flew down to the seas and the oceans, and started painting them blue. Which took them hundreds and hundreds of years, for the seas and the oceans hold a lot of water.

Finally the job was done. But the angels still had a lot of paint left. So God told them, "Take that leftover paint and paint the sky blue."

Which is what they did. And this took hundreds and hundreds of years, for lots of sky is up there.

When the angels finally finished, God said, "Well done! Things look a lot better. Now the seas and oceans are colored the way they should be."

Well, as I told you, maybe this is what happened. The Bible doesn't say it happened that way. I'm just making it up. But don't you wonder sometimes why the sky is blue? Why it is blue rather than some other color?

What if the sky were green? I don't know about you, but a green sky would make my stomach hurt.

Or what if the sky were black? That would make me feel sad all day. You would meet me and ask, "Is something the matter? You look so sad!" And then I would say, "It's the sky! It's the color of the sky! It's all that black up there!"

Or what if the sky were white? That would blind us, wouldn't it? If the sky were white we would have to wear sunglasses all day.

So aren't you glad the sky is blue, the way it is right now? Aren't you glad that God always picks the right colors?

2

God Is Like a Mother Chicken

When I was your age I spent my summer vacations on my uncle's farm. There I learned a lot about horses and cows and porcupines and mice and . . . chickens.

In those days chickens were not cooped up the way they are now. They ran loose all over the place. No matter where you went there was a chick chick here and a chick chick there, here a chick, there a chick, everywhere a chick chick.

As a little boy I loved to get my hands on a baby chick and feel its soft feathers. Plenty of these baby chicks were walking around, but they always stayed close to their mothers.

One day I was lucky. I spotted a baby chick all by itself. I thought, "Here's my chance." I slowly backed it into a corner and was about to grab it when, out of nowhere, the mother chicken came straight toward me, cackling at the top of her lungs and flapping her wings.

When she reached me, she went for my throat. Which was not difficult to do because I was only a little boy and therefore low to the ground. I remember thinking, "Hey, this chicken wants to see blood!" I was scared silly and ran for my life.

Since that time, I've always left plenty of room between any mother chicken and me because I learned that you don't mess with mother chickens.

Why am I telling you this? Because the Bible says that God is like a mother chicken and that you are God's little chick. And because you are, God will fight for you if someone tries to hurt you. That's good to know, don't you agree?

3

Listen to Your Own Voice!

Once upon a time a boy named Tom had a very loud voice, a voice that was a hundred times louder than your voice and my voice. When Tom spoke in a normal tone, all the windows rattled. When he raised his voice, all the windows shattered. When he shouted, people living in Chicago could hear him.

The people who lived on Tom's street often said, "Why does he speak so loud? If only he could hear himself the way we hear him."

But the person who suffered the most was Tom's mother. Tom was always calling her. From the time he got out of bed until he went to bed, Tom would call, "Mom, I want this!" or "Mom, I want that!" He never got anything for himself.

Tom's mother would always say, "Please, Tom, not so loud! If only you could hear yourself the way I hear you!"

One night the weather suddenly turned cold, freezing cold. It turned so cold that it must have been a hundred degrees below zero. And you know how cold that is. When it is a hundred degrees below zero the words you speak freeze as soon as they leave your mouth.

That night Tom woke up shivering because he always slept with his bedroom windows wide open. But do you think he got up to close them? Oh no! Spoiled little brat that he was, he called for his mother to close them. He shouted at the top of his lungs, "Mom! Close my windows!"

But his mother never heard him. For no sooner did his shouts leave his mouth than they froze and fell to the floor. It did not take very long before the floor was covered with frozen shouts.

The next morning the sun came out. Slowly it warmed up

Adapted from Kenneth B. Welles, *Children's Sermons* (Philadelphia: West-minster), pp. 116–18. Copyright © 1954, 1982. By permission of Thomas Welles Barber.

Tom's room. As the room got warmer and warmer, the frozen shouts melted and exploded like firecrackers, one after the other so that the whole room was full of shouts.

For the first time in his life, Tom heard himself shout. And it hurt his ears something awful! Then Tom said, "If this is what I sound like all the time, I'd better apologize to a lot of people."

What Tom learned we have to learn too. We must learn to listen to ourselves. We must always ask ourselves, "How do other people hear me? Do my words hurt their ears? Do my words hurt their feelings?"

4

Harvest Is Coming

Every summer in the wheat fields of America many sad things happen. They don't happen to people, but they do happen to field mice.

Field mice think wheat fields are the best place to live. Everything is free. You don't have to pay to live there. You don't have to pay to eat there. Wheat fields are also fun places. Wouldn't you love to play hide-and-seek among the tall stalks of wheat? And wheat fields are safe places. There is no traffic—no cars, no buses, no trucks. You just couldn't ask for a better place to live.

So you can understand that field mice are very happy animals. Until the harvest. When harvest time comes, big machines move into the wheat fields. Not only do these machines make a lot of noise, they also mow down the wheat, so all of a sudden all those tall wheat stalks come crashing down on the little mice's heads.

Adapted from J. B. Phillips, *For This Day*, ed. Denis Duncan (Waco, Tex.: Word, 1974). Used by permission.

When the harvest comes, the field mice suddenly discover that the field and the wheat do not belong to them at all, but to the farmer.

Harvest comes as a big surprise. Not just to the mice but also to many people. For many people live the way field mice do. They eat and work and play and get married and have children as though the world belongs to them. They live as though there is never going to be a harvest.

Now, you can't blame the field mice for not knowing that there is going to be a harvest. Even though they are very cute little animals, they are also very dumb. But we are not dumb. We are people. We should know better.

This world is like a wheat field. It belongs to God. God is the farmer. One day there is going to be a harvest. And when it comes, we'd better be ready.

5

Have Mercy on Me!

The story I am about to tell you is true. It really happened. It happened in England, where there are many tea shops—places where people go to drink tea. Our story takes place in one of those tea shops.

One day a lady entered a tea shop and sat down at a table with two chairs. She ordered a pot of tea and thought about eating some cookies with her tea, cookies that she had in her purse.

Because the tea shop was crowded, a man took the chair across from this lady. He also ordered tea. The woman then read her newspaper, took a cookie from the package on the table, and saw that the man across from her also took a cookie from this package. This really made her angry, but she decided not to say anything.

After a while she took a second cookie. So did the man across from her. This made her even angrier and she looked at him as though to say, "How dare you eat my cookies!"

While she looked at him like that, the man reached for the last cookie, smiled, and offered her half of it.

By this time the woman was about ready to explode. She was furious. Quickly she got up, left, walked to a nearby bus stop and got on a bus. When she opened her purse to pay the bus fare, guess what she saw? Her package of cookies, unopened.

The man hadn't been eating *her* cookies. She had been eating *his* cookies. You can imagine how she felt. Just awful. But it was too late to go back and apologize.

Have you ever been in a situation like that? Have you ever made such a big mess of things that you couldn't begin to clean it up? What do you do in a case like that? The best thing to do is to

Adapted from Walter Brueggeman, Sharon Parks, and Thomas H. Groome, *To Act Justly, Love Tenderly, Walk Humbly: An Agenda for Ministers* (New York: Paulist Press, 1986), p. 6. Used by permission.

take the Bible and look up Psalm 51. There it says, "Have mercy
on me, O God . . . Against you, you only, have I sinned and done
what is evil in your sight."

Remember that. Psalm 51. I'm quite sure that one day you
will need that psalm.

6

Flap Your Wings!

Once upon a time a certain flock of geese went to church
every Sunday morning. There the oldest goose would preach a
sermon. And no matter what the sermon was about it would
always end the same way. The oldest goose would tell the others,
"Remember this. God made you to fly. God gave you wings to
fly. Some day we must leave here and fly to God's beautiful
country. So get ready. Flap your wings. Practice flying."

But do you think these geese listened to him? Not at all. On
Monday they lived just as if they had never been to church on
Sunday. They lived as if they had never heard the sermon. They
did not flap their wings. They did not practice flying. Instead,
they ate a lot and drank a lot and grew fatter and fatter.

Fortunately not every goose did that. A few geese did flap their
wings and practice flying. But all the others? All they did was eat
and drink, go to church on Sunday and listen to the sermon, and
go home again to eat and drink some more.

Things went on like that for many months. Then suddenly it
was winter. The weather turned cold, and snow covered the
ground. All at once there was nothing to eat, and life became
very hard. Then the oldest goose, who always preached on
Sunday, said, "Listen carefully! The time to fly has finally

Adapted from a story by Søren Kierkegaard.

come." He flapped his wings and flew off to God's beautiful country. So did the geese who had been practicing flapping their wings. They too flew off.

But all the other geese fluttered around but could not get off the ground. Their wings were too weak. Their bodies were too fat. And so they had to stay behind.

What about you? Are you like the geese that flew away? Or are you like the geese that stayed behind? Do you flap your wings every day? Do you exercise your faith every day? Do you pray to God every day? I certainly hope you do.

7

Sorry, God, But ...

There once was a girl about your age whose name was Mary. One day her mother said, "Mary, here are two quarters. One is for church, to put in the offering. The other is for you, to buy candy."

You can well imagine how excited Mary was. She clenched one quarter in her left fist and the other in her right fist. And she said, "I'm gonna show these to my best friend, Karen. Maybe her mother will do what my mother did—give her one quarter for church and one quarter for candy."

Then, as fast as she could, Mary ran over to Karen's house. But she ran too fast so that she stumbled and fell. And as she fell, her two fists opened wide and both quarters rolled away.

At first Mary couldn't find either of them, but after searching some more she finally found one. When she did, can you guess what she said? She said, "Oh no! I just lost the quarter my mom gave me to put in the offering. But I'm glad I found the quarter my mom gave me for candy."

That's what Mary said. And we all know that she didn't say the right thing. We all know that what she should have said is, "Oh no! I just lost the quarter my mom gave me for candy. But I'm glad I found the quarter my mom gave me to put in the offering."

That's what Mary should have said. If you had been Mary, that's what *you* would have said, right? Or am I wrong?

8

Ministers and Pulpits

You children may still be young but you have already heard a lot of ministers preach. As you watched all these different ministers, you must have noticed that they all do different things to the pulpit.

Some ministers pound the pulpit a lot. Each time they say something important they hit the pulpit with their fists. Pulpit pounders don't just say, "Stealing is wrong!" No, they say, "STEALING IS WRONG!" Bang, bang, bang. Pulpit pounders don't just say, "Lying is wrong!" No, they say, "LYING IS WRONG!" Bang, bang, bang.

Other ministers walk a lot. They are what I call pulpit walkers. These are the nervous type. They can't stand still a minute. They keep walking back and forth, back and forth. Watching them is like watching a tennis match.

There also are ministers who jump a lot. When I was your age, our church had a jumping minister. My oldest sister called him "The Frog." Every once in a while he would disappear behind the pulpit and then suddenly jump up.

Then there are ministers who lean a lot. Each time they have something important to say they lean on the pulpit and look you straight in the eye, which can be very scary.

That's how ministers differ. But they are all alike in that they all preach the good news that Jesus died for us and rose for us. And as long as they do that it doesn't really matter, does it, whether they pound or walk or jump or lean?

9

Amazing Grace

What am I holding between my two hands? A piece of red glass. But you say, "Oh no, you aren't. You aren't holding a piece of red glass between your hands. There's nothing there. Nothing at all."

You are right, of course. Nothing is there. But all of you have an imagination, don't you? What if you imagine that I am holding a piece of red glass between my hands? Then you can see it, can't you?

Now watch! I am taking this piece of glass and I'm throwing it on the floor. Crash! Now pieces of red glass are all over the floor.

Use your imagination again. Now what am I holding between my two hands? A piece of blue glass. Watch again! I am throwing it on the floor. Crash! Now pieces of blue glass are all over the floor. Crash! Now pieces of yellow glass are all over the floor.

What a mess. What shall we do with all these pieces of broken glass? Sweep them up and throw them into a trash can? That would be one way to get rid of them. But I have a much better idea. Why not use all these pieces of broken glass and make them into a picture? Why not make them into a colored glass window?

OK, we're ready. Isn't it amazing what you can do with pieces of broken glass? You can turn them into a beautiful colored glass window.

God does the same with us. We are like broken glass. But rather than throw us away, God takes us into his hands and turns us into something beautiful for him.

Look! There's no more glass on the floor. All the pieces are gone. They're all part of this beautiful colored glass window. Amazing, isn't it? Amazing grace—that's what it is!

10

Sometimes It Takes an Odd Bird

Last week I went for a walk. As I was walking down a road where nobody lives, a bird suddenly began to sing. It took me a while to spot the bird, but finally I did. She was a beautiful bird. Her feathers were blue. Her head was white with purple dots here and there. Her tail was bright orange. Her legs were yellow. Her beak was black, which, I understand, is rather unusual. And there was something else unusual about this bird. She had eyelashes.

I patiently waited for the bird to finish her song. Then I talked to her. I said, "I'm sorry, but I don't know your name. My teachers never taught me. They did teach me the names of such ordinary birds as robins and sparrows and bluejays. But they never taught me your name. Sorry about that. Tell me something. Why did you sing this beautiful song in a place where nobody hears you? People who drive past here in cars—they don't hear you. Joggers who run past here with head sets on— they don't hear you. Nobody hears you. You're just lucky I came along. If it hadn't been for me, you would have sung for nothing. You would have wasted your breath. So why don't you sing in places where lots of people can hear you?"

Do you know what the bird said? She said, "Whatever *your* name is, sir, you've got it all wrong. You don't understand. I don't sing for people. I sing for God. God made me to sing for him."

"Thanks," I said.

"Thanks for what?" the bird asked.

"Thanks for reminding me of what the Bible says. The Bible says what you just told me. The Bible says that whoever we are and whatever we do, we must do everything for God."

You know, sometimes it takes an odd bird to remind us of that.

11

Swallowed Alive

What if? What if you were a mouse? What if you were a mouse that lived in the house of a giant? What if that giant loved to eat live mice? What if he loved to eat live mice for breakfast and lunch and dinner and for snacks in between? And what if that giant had set traps all over his house?

Then what? Then you'd better listen to your mom or dad when they tell you to stay away from those traps.

But what if you don't listen? What if you think you know better? What if one day you stick your little mouse head outside the mousehole to see what's going on? And what if you smell cheese? And what if you think, "I want that cheese, and I want it right now"? Then what? Then this is what happens.

You follow the smell of the cheese and discover that it comes from inside a cage. Fortunately, the cage has an opening just your size. So you crawl through the opening, eat the cheese, but then discover that you can't crawl out again. You are trapped.

"Oh no," you think, "how stupid of me. I should have listened!" But it's too late. Pretty soon you hear footsteps. Here comes the giant. He opens the cage, grabs you by the tail, and swallows you alive.

Suddenly you feel as though you are sliding down a long tunnel. And you are. Then, before you know it, you're inside the giant's stomach. You can't see a thing. It smells terrible. It's warm. It's wet. It's scary. Real scary.

You think, "I must get out of here. But how? Who can help me?"

And then you remember something your mom and dad taught you. So you hold your two front paws and pray, "Lord, help me!"

Then something unexpected happens. The giant burps. And burps a second time. And when he burps a third time you are flying through the air. You're out of the giant's stomach, out of the giant's mouth.

As soon as you hit the floor, you run for the mousehole. You're safe. And then you hear your mom's voice, "Where have you been?" When you tell her she says, "Just like Jonah!" "Jonah?" you ask. "Who is Jonah?" Then your mother tells you the story of Jonah. Jonah, like you, did what he shouldn't have done. Jonah got swallowed up, too—not by a giant but by a fish. Jonah prayed for help, too. Jonah was burped up, too.

What if? What if you were that mouse? Then you would understand the story of Jonah much better than anyone else, wouldn't you?

12

Échafaudage

A long, long time ago I took a test in school. Someone had written a story in French. I had to write it in English. That was the test.

I was doing pretty well until I came to a word that I had never seen before. That word was *échafaudage* [pronounced *esh-ah-foh-DAZH*]. I had no idea what it meant.

Come to think of it, the word *échafaudage* sounds a lot like snuffolouphagus. But if you think that snuffolouphagus and *échafaudage* are brother and sister, you are wrong. *Échafaudage* and snuffolouphagus have nothing to do with each other.

So here I was, taking this test and not knowing what the word *échafaudage* meant. Later I asked my friends. They didn't know either.

Well, I passed my test and completely forgot the word *échafaudage*. At least I thought I did. But listen to what happened to me forty-two years later. Forty-two years after I took that test, I was in the part of Switzerland where people speak French. I was riding on a bus when all of a sudden a truck passed by. And can you guess what word was painted on the back of that truck? I looked and said to myself, "I don't believe this! I don't believe this!"

Painted on the back of that truck was the word *échafaudage*— the word I didn't know at my French test forty-two years earlier. I thought I had completely forgotten that word. But I was wrong. Somehow that word had been stored in my brain, but in a part of my brain where I could no longer reach it. But as I saw the word on the back of that truck, I remembered it again.

Our brains are amazing things, aren't they? They store everything we see. They store everything we hear. They store everything we think. How smart God must be to make such brains!

Échafaudage! You know what? Now this French word is stored in your brain too. Whether you like it or not. Isn't that amazing?

13

God's Song

Once upon a time, so an old story goes, God came down to earth to teach his song to the wind and the trees and the brooks and the animals. "Gather around me," God told them, "and I will teach you my song." This took a while, but finally there they all were, standing around God.

Then God sang his song. It was the most beautiful song this world has ever heard.

The wind and the trees and the brooks and the animals—they all listened to God's song. They all tried hard to remember it. But they simply couldn't. It was too hard to remember all of it. All each of them could remember was one part of the song. And that's what they did.

The wind learned to howl. The trees learned to rustle. The brooks learned to babble. The lions learned to roar. The cows learned to moo. The dogs learned to bark. The cats learned to meow. The birds learned to chirp. Each remembered only one part of God's song.

And the fish. Oh yes, let me tell you about the fish, for you may not have heard. Why is it that fish move their mouths but make no sounds? Let me explain. When God sang his song, the fish stuck their eyes and mouths above the water, but not their ears. So they never *heard* God's song. They didn't hear God's voice, but they did see the movement of God's lips. Ever since, that's what they imitate—the movement of God's lips.

The wind, the trees, the brooks and the animals—each learned to sing one part of God's song. When they all sing together they sing the whole song.

Adapted from an ancient Estonian legend.

14

Living in a Shoe

There was an old woman who lived in a shoe.
She had so many children she didn't know what to do;
She gave them some broth without any bread,
She whipped them all soundly and put them to bed.

Do you like this old woman? Probably not. And why not? Because, you say, she spanks her children and children don't like to be spanked.

But perhaps you will like this old woman a lot better after you understand her problems. She has three problems.

Her first problem is that she lives in a shoe. Do you have any idea what that is like? You live in a house. You live in a house that has a roof to keep out the rain and the snow.

But what if you lived in a shoe? What if there was no roof to keep out the rain and the snow? What if there was a big hole instead? What if your dad would say to you one morning, "It snowed last night. Would you please shovel the living room?" Or, "It rained last night. Would you please mop up the living room?"

The old woman has a second problem. She has too many children. And do you know what that is like? Do you have any idea what it is like to be the mother of a large family where the boys are always teasing the girls and the girls are always screaming at the boys? It's enough to give you a splitting headache.

The old woman has one more problem. She has children who are ungrateful. At the end of the day when the children come home tired and hungry, the old woman says, "Children, guess what? I've made you some delicious soup."

And what do her children say? "Soup? Oh no, not again! We had soup yesterday and we had soup the day before yesterday. We've been eating soup for weeks. Can't we have pizza tonight?"

No wonder the old woman gets angry and says, "Shame on you. I've shined the outside of our shoe. I've cleaned your rooms. I've washed your clothes. I've cooked this meal. And now you have the nerve to complain. You deserve to be spanked and to be spanked soundly. To bed, all of you!"

OK, now that you know what the old woman's problems are, don't you like her a little bit better? I'm sure you do. It often works that way. We meet someone we don't like very well. Then we find out about the problems she has, and we like her a lot better.

Can you think of some people you don't like? Do you know what problems they have? Maybe it's time for you to find out what those problems are.

15

What? Why? Where?

Once upon a time lived a man whose name was Do-you-know-what. One day Do-you-know-what met a woman whose name was What-do-you-think. The two fell in love and got married and had a baby—a baby boy. "What shall we name him?" Do-you-know-what asked What-do-you-think. She said, "Let's call him What." And so they did.

When What learned to talk he was always asking *what* questions: "What shall I do?" or "What shall I read?" or "What shall I watch?" or "What shall I wear?"

After some time, Do-you-know-what and What-do-you-think had a second baby. It was a girl. They named her Why. When

Adapted from Kenneth B. Welles, *Children's Sermons* (Philadelphia: Westminster), pp. 28–30. Copyright © 1954, 1982. By permission of Thomas Welles Barber.

Why learned to talk she was always asking *why* questions: "Why is the sky blue?" or "Why is water wet?" or "Why is ice cold?" or "Why is snow white?"

After some time Do-you-know-what and What-do-you-think had a third baby—a baby boy. They named him Where. When Where learned to talk he was always asking *where* questions: "Where did I come from?" or "Where am I going?" or "Where can I find this?" or "Where shall I put that?"

Can you imagine what it was like to live in that family? All day long What was asking *what* questions and Why was asking *why* questions and Where was asking *where* questions. With all their questions the three of them must have driven their parents crazy. Just as you with all your questions must drive your parents crazy.

But keep on asking questions. Keep on asking hard questions. Keep on asking questions like: "What keeps the airplane in the sky?" or "Why can fish breathe under water?" or "Where did I come from?"

Keep asking what, why, and where questions. God wants you to ask them. That's why he gave you a mind.

16

Smart, But Not Wise

Once upon a time lived a man who was very smart. Smart, but not wise. Every day this smart man would go for a long walk and name all the trees and flowers and animals he saw. He would name them, not by their English names, but by their Latin names. That's how smart he was.

One day, on one of his walks, he came to a field that had a large oak tree. On the ground below that tree, pumpkin plants were growing, and the pumpkins were as big as your head. The man thought, "How strange! How strange that a big oak tree grows small acorns and that a small pumpkin grows big pumpkins." The man thought, "God who created the oak tree and the pumpkin plants is not so smart as I thought he was. If I had been God, I would have done things differently. I would have made big pumpkins grow on big trees and small acorns grow on small plants."

Well, this smart but not wise man had done a lot of walking that day, so he decided to rest a while under the big oak tree. "I think I'll take a little nap," he said to himself, and before long he was sound asleep. Just as he was dreaming about how smart he was and how he would have done things differently from the way God had done them, how he would have made big pumpkins grow on big trees and small acorns grow on small plants, just as he was dreaming about that, down fell an acorn, smack on his nose. "Ouch!" the man cried, "What was that?" Then he saw the acorn that had fallen from the tree right onto his nose.

The man thought, "What if pumpkins grew on trees? What if a pumpkin had fallen on my nose? What would have happened then? Then the pumpkin would have smashed my nose!"

Adapted from Kenneth B. Welles, *Children's Stories* (Philadelphia: Westminster), pp. 26–28. Copyright © 1954, 1982. By permission of Thomas Welles Barber.

As he rubbed his nose the man said, "I hate to admit it, but God is smarter and wiser than I am."

And when he said that, he was both smart and wise.

17

Stay Where You Are

Some time ago I read a story. It goes like this. Once upon a time, in a small village, lived a poor man. His name was Isaac. And Isaac lived in a hut.

One night Isaac had a dream. In his dream he was told that if he traveled to a faraway city, he would find a bag of gold under the bridge in the middle of that city.

When Isaac woke up from his dream he said to himself, "I wish dreams were true, but they aren't. Dreams are just dreams."

Still, Isaac kept thinking about his dream. He thought, "What if my dream is true, after all? Some dreams in the Bible were true. Why can't my dream be true? Besides, what do I have to lose? I'm as poor as a church mouse. If I find the bag of gold, I will be rich. If I don't find it, nothing changes and I will stay poor. So what do I have to lose?"

So the next day he began his trip to the faraway city. He traveled for several days. When he finally reached the city, he went right to the bridge in the middle of the city. But when he got there he found that it was guarded by soldiers. No way could he get under the bridge and start digging for the bag of gold.

So guess what Isaac did? He went up to one of the soldiers who was guarding the bridge and told him his dream. And can you guess what the soldier told Isaac? The soldier told him, "You fool! Last night I dreamed that if I traveled to a small village, I would find a treasure behind the fireplace in a hut of a poor man by the name of Isaac."

When Isaac heard that he hurried home and found that the soldier was right. He found a treasure behind his fireplace.

What does this story mean? Can you guess? It means that the great treasures of your life are hidden, not in faraway places but right where you live. It means that the great treasures of your life are as close to you as your home and as your church. It means that the great treasures of your life are right where you live every day and right where you worship every Sunday.

Can you name some of these treasures?

18

Pig Love

You know the story of the three little pigs. Your mom or dad must have told you a hundred times how the wolf blew down the pig's house made of straw, and how the wolf blew down the house made of wood, and how the wolf just couldn't blow down the house made of brick.

What did the wolf do then? Then, so your mom or dad told you, the wolf climbed on top of the roof, slid down the chimney and right into a pot of boiling water.

That's a strange ending to the story, don't you think? Have you ever seen a wolf climb on top of a roof and slide down a chimney? Santa Claus does that sort of thing. Wolves don't.

So what did happen? What did the wolf do after he failed to blow down the brick house? You know what he did? He said to himself, "Those three little pigs are smarter than I thought." And went home.

And for the wolf that was the end of the story. But not for the three little pigs. For them it was just the beginning. By now they hated the wolf. They hated him so much they couldn't think about anything else. They thought they saw the wolf behind every tree. They thought they heard the wolf trying to blow down every house on their street. They thought they heard the wolf howl every hour of the day and night. They went to bed thinking about the wolf and they got up thinking about the wolf. Finally, they said, "This can't go on. We need help and we need it badly."

So they went to see a doctor. And this is what the doctor told them. He said, "You hate the wolf so much, you can't think of anything else. You must stop hating the wolf and begin loving him. When you do, you will soon be the happy little pigs you used to be."

Adapted from a forgotten source.

That sounded like good advice and so the three little pigs paid the doctor one hundred dollars and went home. When they came home they said, "But how can we do that? How can we stop hating the wolf and begin loving him?"

"I know how," the first little pig said. "I'm going to the public library and read all the books on love I can find. After I am finished reading, I will know how to love the wolf."

So that's what she did. She read everything about love. But when she was finished, she still did not feel love for the wolf. She hated him as much as she did before.

The second little pig read in the newspaper that a famous preacher was coming to town to preach three sermons on love. She went to hear the preacher and became very excited about loving other animals. But the next day she wasn't excited anymore and hated the wolf as much as she did before.

The third little pig went across the street to an Old Animals Home. "Maybe I can be of some help there," she thought. And sure enough! Someone asked her to take an old wolf for a ride in his wheelchair.

And guess who that old wolf was. The same wolf who, years ago, had tried to blow her house down.

Things were different now. The old wolf had huffed and puffed too much during his lifetime and now had a hard time breathing. He needed to be wheeled around. He needed to be fed. And that's what the third little pig did. And after she had done that she tucked him in and gave him a kiss smack on his nose.

Then she went home and told the other little pigs. And from that day on the three little pigs visited the wolf every day and came to love him more and more, until they stopped hating him altogether. And so, where once there had been hatred there now was love.

That's a true story. At least, I hope it is. At least, I think it should be.

19

Hey Diddle Diddle

Hey diddle diddle
The cat and the fiddle,
The cow jumped over the moon;
The little dog laughed
To see such sport,
And the dish ran away with the spoon.

You know this nursery rhyme, don't you? You must have heard it at least a hundred times.

But do you know what it means? Probably not, for it sounds like a lot of nonsense. Can a cat play a fiddle? Can a cow jump over the moon? Have you ever heard a dog laugh? Have you ever seen a dish run away with a spoon?

I'm quite sure you haven't. Things like that don't happen in real life. Things like that happen only in your imagination, when you close your eyes and think crazy thoughts. But then as soon as you open your eyes, all those crazy thoughts are gone, and you are back in the world where cats eat mice, and the moon is far away, and dogs bark and bite.

The person who made up "Hey diddle diddle" had a big imagination. She dreamed of a wonderful world. She dreamed of a world where cats no longer kill mice but play the fiddle instead. She dreamed of a world where heaven is so close that even a cow can jump over the moon. She dreamed of dogs laughing instead of barking and biting.

You know what? The Bible dreams of the same kind of world. The Bible dreams of a world where animals don't kill each other but live together peacefully. The Bible dreams of a world where heaven is so close you can touch it.

You know something else? The Bible doesn't just dream about such a world. It promises that one day you will live in that kind of world.

That gives you something to look forward to, doesn't it?

20

Rejoice, Give Thanks, and Sing

Once a man whose name was Plumptre, Edward Plumptre, liked to sing. So did his wife. They sang in the morning. They sang in the afternoon. They sang in the evening. They sang all day. They sang every day.

Mr. and Mrs. Plumptre had three children. The name of their first child was Rejoice, the name of their second child was Give Thanks, and the name of their third child was Sing. Three children: Rejoice, Give Thanks, and Sing.

Once, after the Plumptre family had moved to a new town and the first Sunday came around, Mrs. Plumptre said, "Let's go to church!" "Yeah!" everyone said, "Let's rejoice, give thanks, and sing!" So the whole Plumptre family went to church.

The name of the minister of the church they went to was Sing Softly, the Reverend Sing Softly. The Reverend Sing Softly wanted every member in his church to sing softly because, he said, it sounded much better that way. Most people, he said, don't know how to sing well, and when you don't know how to sing well you sound much better singing softly than singing loudly.

To sing softly, some people sang out of the right side of their mouths while others sang out of the left side of their mouths. Still others sang through their noses, and rumors went around that a few even sang through their ears.

Here was the Plumptre family, sitting on the front row, ready to sing. When the minister said, "Let's sing hymn 561, 'Rejoice, Ye Pure in Heart,'" all five members of the Plumptre family said, "Yeah, let's do that." Then they stood up and sang the hymn loudly.

Adapted from Kenneth B. Welles, *Children's Sermons* (Philadelphia: Westminster), pp. 60–62. Copyright © 1954, 1982. By permission of Thomas Welles Barber.

This really surprised the people in church. They wondered, "Who are these people? Don't they know how to sing? Don't they know how to sing softly?"

But the loud singing of the Plumptre family sounded so good! So after the first verse of the hymn, everybody started to sing a little bit louder. And after the second verse they sang even louder. And you should have heard them sing the fifth verse! What was especially amazing was that the Reverend Sing Softly sang louder than everybody else.

His church grew to be the rejoicest, give thanksest, and singingest church in town.

Now I can hear you say, "That's just a story. It really didn't happen that way." But are you sure? Ask your mom or dad to get out a hymnbook and look up "Rejoice, Ye Pure in Heart." Then ask them to read what it says about the person who wrote the hymn. It says that the words of the hymn were written by Mr. Edward Plumptre. And then ask your mom or dad to read to you the first verse of that hymn. It reads, "Rejoice, ye pure in heart, rejoice, give thanks, and sing." These are the names of the three Plumptre children, aren't they? So you see, the story of the Plumptre family is truer than you think it is.

21

Swallowing Junk

How many stomachs do you have? Only one! How many stomachs does a cow have? Four! "That's not fair," I can hear you say. "Why should I have only one stomach and any dumb cow has four?"

Good question. Actually, you're much better off having only one stomach. If you had four stomachs, you would have to live like a cow, and I don't think you would like that.

Let me explain. When *you* eat, you chew your food before you swallow it. When a *cow* eats, she swallows her food before she chews it. That's why she needs three extra stomachs. She needs them to store the food she swallowed before she chewed.

Because a cow swallows her food in a hurry, she swallows a lot of junk along with it. Junk like buttons and keys and pocket knives and wristwatches and spoons. And I'm not kidding you. I once read a story of an animal doctor who operated on cows and found all these things in their stomachs: buttons, keys, pocket knives, wristwatches, and spoons.

Even though people have only one stomach and must chew their food before they can swallow it, many behave just like cows. They swallow any junky thing that comes along. They listen to gossip and swallow it. They listen to nasty stories and swallow them. They watch trashy TV programs and swallow them.

When you swallow all these junky things, you are just like a dumb cow. When you swallow all that junk, it will make you sick.

The Bible says, Before you chew something, first taste it. Before you swallow something, first chew it. If it's bad, spit it out. If it's good, eat it. Which sounds like good advice, don't you think?

22

Pihi Birds

Every bird has two wings. To fly, every bird needs two wings.
But there is one bird that has only one wing. It's called the Pihi
(pronounced peehee) bird.

A Pihi bird is not a real bird. It's a story bird. It lives only in
stories. It flies only in stories, in Chinese stories.

The Pihi bird has only one wing. The father Pihi bird has a
right wing and the mother Pihi bird a left wing. Or just the other
way around. I can't remember. The important thing to remember
is that father and mother Pihi can fly only if they work together.

Let's think about that for a while. Let's think about what
father and mother Pihi would talk about while flying together.

Father Pihi is saying to mother Pihi, "Dear, you're not doing
your share. For the past hour we've been flying in circles. I have
been flapping my wing faster than you have. So could you please
flap your wing a little bit faster?"

Mother Pihi answers back, "No, I can't. I'm too tired. I've been
taking care of our twelve little Pihis all day. Do you have any
idea what that takes out of me?"

Father Pihi then says, "What do you think I've been doing all
day? Sitting on a branch? Teasing cats? Looking at other birds?
No, I've been catching worms all day. You think I like doing
that? I hate worms. They make me gag. They're slimy and sticky.
When I was young, my mother stuffed worms down my throat all
day long. She told me they were good for me."

It's not easy being a Pihi. It's not easy to fly together. But to
get anywhere, that's what Pihis have to do.

It's not easy being a Christian either. It's not easy to do things
with others. But to get anywhere, that's what Christians have to
do. They must pray together. They must sing together. They
must worship together.

That's why we go to church every Sunday.

23

Volcanoes

Do you know what a volcano is? A volcano, you could say, is a burning mountain. Deep down inside of it there is a burning fire, a fire that wants to get out. And when it does, you'd better not be anywhere around. For when a volcano explodes, it spits out smoke and ashes and rocks and lava.

"Lava?" you ask, "What is lava?" Lava is melted rock that is ten times as hot as boiling water and as thick as the chocolate sauce you put on your ice cream.

When a volcano explodes, lava comes flowing down the mountainside. After the lava cools off, it turns into hard rock.

A long time ago I went to see a volcano somewhere in Japan. This volcano hadn't exploded for many years, so it was quite safe to go near it. What I saw surprised me. I saw nothing but lava, lava as far as I could see, lava that had killed everything green— the grass, the flowers, the bushes, the trees.

Some people are just like a volcano, just like a burning mountain. Deep down inside them there is a burning fire, a burning anger. This anger wants to get out. And when it does, you'd better not be anywhere around. When angry people explode, words as hot as lava come flowing from their lips. These angry words do a lot of damage. They hurt a lot of people.

Angry people have few friends. People avoid them. People are afraid to come near them. What does the Bible say to people who are angry? It tells them: Never go to bed angry. Get rid of your anger before you go to sleep.

There's nothing wrong with being angry for a little while. For example, when your little brother smashes your new watch with a hammer, it's perfectly OK for you to be angry at him. Or when your sister takes a handful of butter and rubs it into your hair, it's perfectly OK for you to be angry at her.

But don't stay angry. Don't go to bed angry. You may turn into a little volcano.

24

Angels and Children

Once upon a time an angel ran past a big church. The minister of that church happened to see the angel. He stuck his head out of the window and shouted, "Wait! There's something I'd like to ask you, something about my church." But the angel shouted back, "I don't have time for your church. I'm on my way to something more important. Your church must wait till later." And the angel ran on.

The minister said, "I'd like to find out what's more important than my church." So he followed the angel.

Next the angel ran past the king's palace. The king too happened to see the angel. He stuck his head out of the window and shouted, "Wait! There's something I'd like to ask you, something about my kingdom." But the angel shouted back, "I don't have time for your kingdom. I'm on my way to something more important. Your kingdom must wait till later." And the angel ran on.

The king said, "I'd like to find out what's more important than my kingdom." So he too followed the angel.

The angel ran down Main Street and then turned onto a side street. Here a little boy stood crying his heart out. He had lost his mother. The angel ran up to him, hugged him, and said, "It's all right! All you did was turn the wrong corner. Your mother is just around the corner. Look, here she comes right now."

And sure enough. A woman came running toward them. The angel put the little boy in his mother's arms and was about to go back to God when he saw the minister and the king. They were huffing and puffing and staring at the little boy in his mother's arms.

Adapted from Kenneth B. Welles, *Children's Sermons* (Philadelphia: Westminster), pp. 17–19. Copyright © 1954, 1982. By permission of Thomas Welles Barber.

Can you guess what the angel said to them? He said, "Now that I have solved this big problem, may I help you solve your little problems? Tell me, what are they?"

What this story means is that just because grownups are big doesn't mean that their problems are big too. And just because you boys and girls are small doesn't mean that your problems are small too. To God, some of your problems are much bigger than those of grownups.

25

The Story of the Good Eel

Once upon a time, in the middle of the ocean, a fish was swimming all by itself. Suddenly sharks came and began to attack the fish. They tore off many of its scales. They bit it in several places. Then they went away, leaving the fish half dead.

After a while, some tuna fish came swimming along. They all looked at the fish and felt sorry for it. The oldest of the tuna fish said, "What is happening to our beautiful ocean? We used to be able to swim safely anywhere. Not any more!" But none of the tuna fish stopped to help the poor injured fish. They all swam on past it.

After a while, some whitefish came along. They too looked at the fish and felt sorry for it. The oldest whitefish said, "Dumb fish! It should never have swum here by itself. That's asking for trouble. Every fish with a little bit of brains knows that the middle of the ocean is a dangerous place, a very dangerous place." But none of the whitefish stopped to help the poor fish. They all swam on past it.

Adapted from a story by Robert McAfee Brown that appeared in *The Christian Century*.

After a while, an electric eel came along. When he saw the poor fish he felt sorry for it, swam up to it, gave it an electric shock to bring it back to life, and then wrapped himself around the fish and slowly dragged it to a cave, where the fish would be safe from sharks.

Now, in this cave lived an octopus. The electric eel swam up to her and asked, "Mrs. Octopus, could you please hold this poor fish in one of your eight arms? And could you hold it there until it is better? Here are some yummy oysters to pay for your services." Then the electric eel swam away.

My question is: If right now you would turn into a fish, which fish would you like to turn into? Would you like to turn into a shark, or into a tuna fish, or into a whitefish, or into an electric eel? Did I hear you say that you would like to turn into an electric eel? You have answered well.

26

Pecking Order

When I was a little boy, I spent summer vacations on my uncle's farm. On that farm there were many chickens, all running loose. Chickens don't do that nowadays. Today, chickens are all cooped up. Not in those days. Anywhere you walked you ran into chickens. There was a chick chick here and a chick chick there, here a chick, there a chick, everywhere a chick.

As you can understand, I learned a lot about chickens. For example, I learned that some chickens are higher than others. I learned that higher chickens are allowed to peck lower chickens but that lower chickens are not allowed to peck higher chickens. I learned that there is a certain order in which chickens may peck others. It's called a pecking order.

At the top is Chicken Number One. Chicken Number One may peck any chicken in sight. But none of the chickens may peck Chicken Number One. Right below Chicken Number One is Chicken Number Two. Chicken Number Two may peck any chicken in sight, any chicken except Chicken Number One. None of the chickens may peck Chicken Number Two, none except Chicken Number One.

And so on down the line, until you get to the bottom of the pecking order where there is a chicken that all the other chickens may peck but which may not peck any chicken at all. This poor chicken at the bottom of the pecking order has lost most of her feathers and has bloody spots all over her body.

I have learned that boys and girls often behave the same way chickens do. I have learned that children too have a pecking order. At the top of the pecking order is Boy Number One. He is the bully on the school bus. He threatens everyone who is smaller and weaker than he is. He says nasty things about everyone else, but no one is allowed to say nasty things about him.

Or at the top of the pecking order is Girl Number One. She

makes unkind remarks about everybody else's clothes or hair, but don't you dare make any unkind remark about her clothes or hair!

Right below Boy or Girl Number One is Boy or Girl Number Two, and so down the line, until way at the bottom of the pecking order you find a boy or girl who doesn't have a single friend.

When boys and girls behave like pecking chickens, it is sad. But when boys and girls who are Christians behave like pecking chickens, it is doubly sad. For being a Christian means that you behave like Jesus. And Jesus always stuck up for people at the bottom of the pecking order. Jesus always became their friend.

So should we, don't you agree?

27

The Story of Two Clocks

Once upon a time there was an old clock. This clock went tick, tock, tick, tock very slowly and very sadly. When it struck the hour, it seemed to say, "Let's all be sad! Let's all be very sad! Another hour has just died and is gone forever!"

One day a new clock moved into the same room. It was a pretty little clock and ticked very quickly and very joyfully. It went tick, tick, tick, tick.

When this new clock struck the hour it seemed to say, "Let us rejoice and be glad! A new hour has just been born!"

As you can well imagine, the old clock didn't like the new clock one little bit. "You are a clock?" the old clock asked. "You certainly don't sound like one. You sound more like an eggbeater."

The new clock said, "Sorry, but that's the way I tick." "Don't be silly," the old clock said. "There is only one way to tick, and that is my way, the slow way. You tick too fast."

"But what difference does that make?" the new clock asked. "What difference does it make whether I tick fast or slow, just so long as I tell the right time?"

For the next few days the two clocks didn't talk to each other. All they did was tick—the old clock slowly, the new clock quickly.

Then one sunny morning the old clock spoke. "Little clock," it said, "I have been thinking things over. You were right and I was wrong. It does not matter how you tick. The only thing that matters is that you tell the right time. So let's be friends." And then to celebrate their friendship the two clocks struck the hour together.

Now, my question is: Who is the new clock and who is the old clock? The answer is not hard to guess. You are the new clock and your mom and dad are the old clock. For you and they are different. The way you tick is different from the way they tick. Which is OK, just as long as you tell the same time, just as long as you worship the same God, just as long as you love the same Jesus.

For the rest? Why, you children are free to tick any way you want.

28

Tomorrow Will Be Monday

As Tommy Snooks and Bessy Brooks
Were walking out one Sunday,
Said Tommy Snooks to Bessy Brooks,
"Tomorrow will be Monday."

You probably know this nursery rhyme. But do you know what it means? "Yes," you say, "I know what it means. You see, Tommy Snooks is taking a walk with Bessy Brooks on Sunday. And because Tommy Snooks has never taken a walk with a girl before, he blushes each time he looks at her and has a hard time knowing what to say to her. And so he says dumb things like: 'You know what, Bessy? Today is Sunday, right? Well, that means tomorrow will be Monday.' "

That, you may say, is what Tommy Snooks means when he says, "Tomorrow will be Monday." And you may very well be right.

Now, let me tell you what I think Tommy Snooks means. It is Sunday morning. Church is over. On his way home from church Tommy Snooks spots Bessy Brooks and asks her to go for a walk with him.

As they walk, they talk. They talk about church and about the sermon they just heard. And then Tommy Snooks says to Bessy Brooks, "You know, Bessy, it's easy to be a Christian on Sunday. It's easy to go to church and listen to a sermon. It's hard to be a Christian on Monday when you have to go back to school. It's harder to be a Christian on Monday than it is on Sunday."

Could that have been what Tommy Snooks meant when he said, "Tomorrow will be Monday"? What do you think?

29

Stick Like a Burr

When we were little boys, my brother and I used to spend our summer vacation on our uncle's farm. One of the things we did was throw burrs at each other.

Do you know what burrs are? Burrs are round, rough, and prickly things that grow on certain plants and that stick to your clothes like crazy.

One time my brother and I got into real trouble throwing burrs. Every summer, in the month of August, a big threshing machine would come to the farm across the road from my uncle's farm. We would go over there and watch it. But after a while that gets to be pretty boring. So one time my brother and I decided to have some fun and throw burrs at the people running that threshing machine. For a while they didn't mind. But then they told us to cut it out. Which we didn't. We kept throwing burrs at them.

Finally they had enough of it and came after us. They took the burrs we had and rubbed them into our hair. Which was a mean thing to do. For burrs stick. Burrs stick like crazy. It took us the rest of the day to get these miserable things out of our hair.

The reason I am telling you this story is because it reminds me of a beautiful burr story. Have you ever heard of Martin Luther? Hundreds of years ago Martin Luther made many changes in the church. The name of Luther's wife was Catherine. She died when she was fifty-one years old. The last words she spoke were: "I will stick to Christ like a burr to a coat."

I hope you do too—stick to Christ like a burr to a coat.

30

Does Church Last Too Long?

Do you think church lasts too long? If you think it does, you can be thankful that you and your mom or dad aren't Puritans living in New England some three hundred years ago. For in those days church lasted quite a bit longer than it does today.

In the days of the Puritans, ministers preached for two or three hours. If your minister would preach that long, you would be climbing the walls or tearing the hymnal into small pieces.

In the days of the Puritans, ministers also prayed long prayers. Some prayed for as long as an hour. If your minister would pray that long, I don't know what you would do. Maybe you would be standing on your head or tearing your hair out.

Because the Puritans had to listen to these long sermons and these long prayers, many of them fell asleep during church. Do you know what they did to keep people from falling asleep? One of the people in church would go around with a long pole. On one end of this pole was a hard knob. The pole man would rap the head of every man or boy who fell asleep.

On the other end of the pole was a rabbit's foot or a squirrel's tail. With it the pole man would tickle the face of every women or girl who fell asleep.

Next time you go to church and think church lasts too long, look at your mom or dad and then say softly to yourself, "Am I glad we aren't Puritans living three hundred years ago! If we were, who knows what I might be doing right now."

31

The Lame and the Blind

Once upon a time, in a faraway country, lived a king. One day he invited all the people in his kingdom to come and eat with him. "On the first day of next month, at 12 o'clock sharp," the king said, "I want everybody to be my guest at a special dinner in my palace. But be on time. If you aren't, you will be turned away."

To make it on time, some people had to travel for several days. One of these was a lame man. One evening he stopped at an inn and sat down next to another traveler. The lame man said, "I'll never make it in time for the king's special dinner. My legs cannot move that fast."

The other traveler said, "I am on the way to the king's special dinner, too, but I'm even worse off than you are. I am blind. That makes me walk very, very slowly."

Now, a third traveler heard what the lame man and the blind man said to each other. He said, "The reason you two men are not going to make it in time for the special dinner is because you are trying to get there on your own. If only you would travel together, I'm sure you could get there on time."

"But how?" the lame man and the blind man asked. "Very simple," the other traveler answered. "You, blind man, can walk, right? Then why don't you carry the lame man on your back? And you, lame man, can see, right? Then why don't you tell the blind man where to walk?"

And that's what they did. The blind man carried the lame man on his back and the lame man told the blind man where to walk. By doing things together they arrived at the king's special dinner on time.

This story reminds me of the church. What is the church? The church is like the lame man and the blind man traveling together. By traveling together and helping each other they make it in time for God's special dinner.

32

Prayer Is a Window

Once upon a time a man lived in a house without a window. Naturally, it was very dark inside his house.

One day he said to himself, "I'm sick and tired of living in a dark house. I want to get rid of the darkness. I want light instead of darkness."

So what did he do? He took a large pail, filled it with darkness, carried it outside, and emptied it. Then he went back into the house and did the same thing all over again. He filled the pail with darkness, carried it outside, and emptied it. He did this all day. But by the end of the day his house was just as dark as it had always been.

Then the man said to himself, "This isn't going to work. This is not the way to get rid of the darkness. There must be another way. But how?"

That night he went to bed, very tired and very sad. But when he woke up the next morning, the answer came to him. "Now I know how to get rid of the darkness," he said. He took a big hammer, knocked a big hole in the outside wall, and made a window. Through this window the bright sunlight came pouring into his house.

Our lives are like a house without a window. It's dark inside. To make it light inside, we need a window, a window through which God's light will come pouring into our lives.

Prayer is such a window. Without prayer, our lives are dark. With prayer, our lives are light. Each time we pray, God's light comes pouring into our lives.

33

Watch Out for the Camel's Nose

Once upon a time a traveler was riding his camel across the desert. Suddenly the sand began to blow. Quickly the traveler jumped off his camel, put up a small tent, and wrapped a cloth over his nose and mouth to keep out the sand.

As he lay in his tent waiting for the sandstorm to blow over, the camel stuck his head inside the tent and said, "Please, master, may I come in?" "Don't be silly," the traveler said, "there's no room for both of us."

"In that case," the camel said, "can I at least keep my nose inside your tent, so I can breathe clean air?" "OK," the traveler said, "Just your nose, no more."

After a while the camel stuck his head inside the tent. "Get out!" the traveler said. "Didn't I tell you, 'Just your nose, no more'?" "Yes, you did," the camel said, "but my head isn't very big, and there is plenty of room for it in this tent." "OK then," the traveler said, "just your head and no more."

After a while the camel began to push his body into the tent so that there was less and less room for the traveler. "I'm getting out of here," the traveler said, "otherwise the camel will crush me."

So in the end the camel was inside the tent and the traveler outside the tent. That's why people who ride camels say, "Watch out for the camel's nose."

A little lie is like a camel's nose. A little lie will stick its nose inside your heart and ask, "May I come in? I'm only a little lie. I won't take much room." Then when you let it in, what happens? You soon discover that another little lie wants to come in, and another, and still another. Until your heart is full of lies.

Watch out for the camel's nose!

An ancient fable from the Middle East.

34

Strange, If . . .

Basketball is a strange game, a very strange game. One of the players catches the ball, but instead of keeping it, throws it away. Another player catches the ball and does the same thing. He throws it away. Nobody wants the ball. Everybody keeps throwing it away.

After a while someone throws the ball into a net. And you think to yourself, "This must be the end of the game." But you are wrong, dead wrong. Someone must have cut a big hole at the bottom of the net, for the ball falls right through. And with the return of the ball the game continues.

The game now moves to the other side of the court. Here someone throws the ball into another net. Again you think, "This must be the end of the game!" But you are wrong again. For that net also has a big hole at the bottom.

Another strange thing about basketball is the person on the side who does a lot of yelling. They call him the coach. All he does is boss people around. And every once in a while he stops the game and chews out the whole team. It makes you wonder, "If he is so smart, if he knows how the game should be played, why doesn't he play himself?" But, no, all he does is yell at the players.

Another strange thing about basketball is the people called referees. They wear striped shirts and look like zebras. They keep messing up the game by blowing their silly whistles.

Basketball is strange—if you don't know the rules. But if you do, it makes sense. Only if you do does basketball make sense.

Church too is strange—if you don't know the rules. In church, people stand up and sit down. They sing and read. They close their eyes and fold their hands. They are quiet and listen.

Very strange, if you don't know the rules. But if you do, church makes sense. Only if you do does church make sense.

35

God Answers Prayer

The story I'm about to tell you is true. Many years ago my friends Rudy and Trina had a baby boy, whom they named Danny.

During the first night home from the hospital something was wrong with the nipple of Danny's bottle. So Trina said to Rudy, "Why don't you go downstairs to the kitchen and get me another nipple?"

So Rudy went downstairs, boiled some water, put a nipple in it so that it wouldn't have any germs on it, took out the nipple with a pair of tongs, carried it upstairs, but dropped it.

Back to the kitchen he went to do the same thing all over again. "Careful now," he told himself, "don't drop that nipple again!" But he did. Back to the kitchen again, doing the same thing one more time. "Don't drop it again, you dummy," he told himself, but he did anyway. But the fourth time he made it and little Danny drank his milk.

But this is not the end of the story. During the first week home Danny kept waking up his mom and dad. Night after night Danny kept them awake until they were so tired they could hardly keep their eyes open.

They decided to pray about it. "Lord," they prayed, "we love little Danny very much. Thank you for giving him to us. But he has been keeping us awake night after night. Now we are very, very tired. Please make Danny sleep through the night so we can get some rest. Amen."

God heard their prayer. The next night Danny slept and slept and never woke up once. And what do you think my friends did? Did they thank God for hearing their prayer? No! They looked at each other and said, "Do you think there is something wrong with Danny? He has never done this before. He has never slept through the night. What if something is the matter with him? We better wake him up, just to make sure."

So they woke poor Danny up. Of course, there was nothing wrong with Danny. There was something wrong with Danny's mom and dad. They did not believe that God would answer their prayer.

Aren't we all like Danny's mom and dad? We pray to God. God answers our prayer. But we don't quite trust the answer.

When we do things like that, God must think we are really strange. And we are!

36

Being Lost

Have you ever been lost in the city? I have. Once I was lost in the city of Boston, trying to find Park Street. So I asked a gentleman, "Sir, can you tell me how to get to Park Street?"

He mumbled a few directions that turned out to be wrong. For when I followed them, I ended up in a cemetery, a place full of dead people. Looking around me I said to myself, "This can't be right."

Next I asked a woman, "Ma'am, can you tell me how to get to Park Street?" She was very helpful and gave detailed directions. She said, "Take the first street on your right, then the second street on your left. Go past a big church and cross the bridge. Here the road forks. Follow the road going to your left, then turn right after two blocks, and Park Street will be the fourth street to your right. You can't miss it."

Well, I did miss it. By the time I got to the big church I had forgotten the rest of her directions. There were too many of them.

Then I asked a college student with a long beard and messy hair. "Can you tell me how to get to Park Street?" He said, "Yes,

I can. But it's not easy. So why don't I just walk you there."
Which is what he did and that's how I got to Park Street.

When you ask people how to find God, you get the same kind
of answers. Some people will give you wrong directions. When
you follow them you end up in a place full of dead people.

Other people will give you too many directions. They tell you,
"First do this, then that. Make sure you don't do this or that will
happen. And be careful not to do this for otherwise you'll end up
doing that."

But then there are people who, like the student with the long
beard and messy hair, don't just tell you the way but show you
the way.

Jesus does that. He shows you the way to God. In fact, he is
the way to God. When you ask him, "How can I find God?" he
points to himself and says, "I am the way to God."

37

Together We Are a Body

What if? What if you are playing outside and a nose walks past you? Not someone with a nose, but a nose without someone. Not a woman with a nose, but a nose without a woman. Or not a man with a nose, but a nose without a man. If that would happen you'd be scared wouldn't you?

Or what if you are playing inside with your toys and all of a sudden two hands appear and start moving the furniture around? Or start playing the piano? What would you do? Keep playing with your toys? I don't think so. I think you would turn pale and run toward your mom or dad.

Or what if tonight, right after you go to bed, a mouth appears. Not someone with a mouth, but a mouth without someone. And what if that mouth would say, "I want you to go to sleep right away. Tomorrow will be another busy day for you." Would you do what the mouth tells you? Would you go to sleep right away? I don't think so. I think you would be so scared, you would not sleep all night.

Or what if you are sitting in church and a pair of legs would come walking down the aisle and sit down right next to you. What would you do? Smile at those legs and say, "Hi"? I don't think so. I think you would jump up and scream.

And why? Why be afraid of legs, or of hands, or of a mouth, or of a nose? Because legs and hands and mouths and noses are not supposed to be all by themselves. They are supposed to be part of a body. And if they are not, if they are not part of a body, then something is terribly wrong.

Now think of the church you go to as a body. And think of all the people in church as parts of the body. One person is the hands and plays the organ, or collects money. Another person is the voice and sings in the choir, or preaches. Still another person is the legs and visits sick people in the hospital.

Can one person do all these things? Can one person play the

organ and sing in the choir and preach and collect money and visit sick people? Of course not. But together many people can.

The hands cannot say to the nose, "I don't need you." And the mouth cannot say to the legs, "I don't need you." They all need each other. Together they are a body. Together we are the body of Christ.

38

Topsy-Turvy

Once upon a time lived an angel who was neither big nor small, but somewhere in between, like most angels are. What made him different from the rest was that he flew upside down. Not rightside up like all the other angels, but upside down. And because he flew upside down, the other angels called him Topsy-Turvy, for *topsy-turvy* means upside down.

Because Topsy-Turvy flew upside down, he bumped into a lot of angels. When he did, he always said, "I'm sorry," for he was very polite. And so were the other angels. They never said, "Topsy-Turvy, would you please look where you are flying? Why don't you fly rightside up, like everybody else does?"

One day, however, things went a little bit too far. The angels had choir practice and Topsy-Turvy was late. Because he was late, he bumped into almost every choir angel before he finally found his place.

Then the angel choir director asked him, "Topsy-Turvy, what's the big idea? Do you have to fly upside down and bump into everybody? Do you have to be different from the rest of us?"

Topsy-Turvy answered, "Yes, I do. It is my job to remind everybody that in the kingdom of God everything is upside down. In the kingdom of people, people hate their enemies. But in the kingdom of God, people love their enemies. In the kingdom of people, everybody wants to be the greatest. But in the kingdom of God, everybody wants to be the least. By flying upside down, I remind everybody that in the kingdom of God things are the opposite of what they are in the kingdom of people."

"Well," the choir director said, "if that's the reason, then by all means keep flying upside down."

And that's what Topsy-Turvy has been doing ever since. So next time you think to yourself, "I sure hate that girl," or "I sure hate that boy," and it feels as though someone is bumping into you, it may very well be Topsy-Turvy reminding you that in the kingdom of God people don't hate each other but love each other.

39

Is Your Mom Mean?

Being a child is not always easy. I'm sure you agree. Being a child can be tough.

Let me give you an example. Let's say you want to draw a beautiful picture on the living room wall with your crayons. So you ask your mom, "Is it OK if I draw a picture on the wall?" But what does your mom say? She says, "Don't you dare! Don't you dare touch that wall with your crayons! You leave that wall alone, do you hear?"

You think to yourself, "If only she could see how beautiful a crayon picture looks on the living room wall, I'm sure she would change her mind in a hurry."

So the next day, when your mom goes grocery shopping, you get out your crayons and draw the most beautiful picture you have ever drawn. Where? On the living room wall. When it is finished you look at it and think, "I can't wait till mom comes home. Will she be surprised!"

When your mom comes home she's surprised all right. But not the way you want her to be. She shouts, "What? Didn't I tell you to leave the living room wall alone?" Then she gives you a sound spanking and sends you to your room.

As I said, being a child can be tough.

But being a parent can be tough too. Let me explain. Some time ago I read a story about a gorilla in a zoo. This gorilla had hurt his head. But instead of leaving his sore head alone, he kept poking at it.

"This has to stop," the zookeeper said. So he took an air gun and every time the gorilla raised his hand to poke at his sore head, the zookeeper would fire small bullets at the gorilla's arm.

Inspired by Proverbs 23:13: "Do not withhold discipline from your children; if you beat them with a rod, they will not die" (NRSV).

Finally, the gorilla left his sore head alone. And it got better in a hurry.

Here is my question: Was the zookeeper mean each time he shot at the gorilla? Of course not!

Here is my next question: Is your mom mean each time she punishes you? Of course not!

40

The Floating Bible

There are many beautiful stories about the Bible. But one of the most beautiful stories is the one I am about to tell you. It happened in Japan, some 140 years ago.

At that time, the Japanese people would not let people from other countries into Japan. No missionaries could come there from other countries. Also, at that time Japanese people were not allowed to be Christians and have Bibles.

The coast of Japan was carefully guarded to make sure that no one would sneak into the country.

Now, one of the persons guarding the Japanese coast was a man by the name of Murata. One day as Murata was standing along the coast, he spotted a book floating on top of the water. When it was close enough, he fished it out. When he tried to read it, he found he couldn't. It was written in a different language.

So Murata went to a person who knew several languages and asked, "Tell me, what language is this book written in and what is this book about?" The person studied the book and said, "It's a Bible written in the Dutch language."

When Murata heard this, he sent someone to China, which is a country not far from Japan, to get a copy of the Bible in the Chinese language. You see, although Murata could not read the

Bible in the Dutch language, he could read it in the Chinese language.

Murata studied his Chinese Bible very carefully for a long time. During that time the laws of Japan changed and missionaries from other countries were now allowed to live in Japan. Finally, ten years after Murata had fished the Dutch Bible out of the sea, he told a missionary that he believed what is written in the Bible and asked the missionary to baptize him.

The Bible is a powerful book. It is powerful even when it comes floating on the water. It is powerful even when it is written in a language you can't understand. Next time you hear the Bible read to you in English, think of how its power changed Murata and how it can change you too.

41

God Is Like a Mother Eagle

Who teaches little eagles how to fly? The mother eagle does. But how does she?

I once read a story written by a person who watched eagles for many days. One day this writer spotted an eagle flying over a mountain valley. It was a mother eagle. On her back she was carrying one of her eaglets. An eaglet is a little eagle.

Suddenly, the mother eagle dropped her eaglet. Down it went. But then it spread its tiny wings and began to fly. The wind was too strong, however, and the young eagle's wings were too weak. So after flapping its wings for a while, it grew tired and began to go down, first slowly, then faster and faster.

In an instant the mother eagle swooped down and caught the little bird on her back. Then the mother eagle took it up again, for a second try. Again she dropped the little eaglet. Again the little eaglet spread its wings. This time it managed to fly a little longer.

But then, again, it grew tired and began to fall. Again the mother eagle saved it. Again it swooped down and caught the little eaglet on her back.

God is just like a mother eagle. God wants us to be free, to be as free as the birds of the air. But being free as a bird is not always easy. Sometimes it makes us very tired. Sometimes the wings of our faith grow very tired. Then we go down. But as we go down, we make a great discovery. We discover that God is there to catch us. God is just like a mother eagle.

42

Are You Afraid of Spiders?

A long time ago, as I was reading a book, a spider came down from the ceiling and stopped right in front of my eyes.

"Hi, there!" I said. "Where did you come from?"

"From the ceiling above you," the spider answered.

"Where are you going?" I asked.

"I don't know," the spider answered. "I honestly don't know." And from the way he said it I could tell that he was very upset.

"I'm lost," the spider said. "I'm lost in your house. I'm lost in the world. I'm lost in the universe. I don't know where to go anymore. Everyone is afraid of me. Everyone hates me. Everyone tries to kill me."

"Wait a minute," I said. "What do you mean 'Everyone is afraid of me. Everyone hates me. Everyone tries to kill me'? I'm not afraid of you. I don't hate you. I'm not trying to kill you."

"Really?" the spider asked. "Then how come you killed one of my friends a week ago when your little girl called from the bathroom, 'Dad, there's a spider here. Can you come and kill it?' Why did you go up and kill it? You have blood on your hands, Mr. Timmer, spider blood!"

Then the spider asked, "Why? Why are all of you people the same? Why do all of you kill spiders? Didn't God create spiders just as much as he created cats and dogs? But I don't see you go around killing cats and dogs. So why go around killing spiders?"

I've thought about this question for a long time. Now I think the spider is right and we are wrong. God did not create spiders so that we might kill them.

Next time you see a spider, don't ask your mom or dad to kill it. Talk to the spider. Say to it, "Let's be friends, distant friends, friends from far away, but friends and not enemies."

The spider will appreciate that very much.

43

Crabby Abby

Have you ever heard the story of Crabby Abby? It's not a very nice story. Still, I think you should hear it.

Once upon a time lived a little girl whose name was Abby. Abby was a pretty girl and a happy girl. Then, one day she found a ten-dollar bill lying on the street. "Wow!" Abby said. "Think of all the candy I can buy now."

From that day on, Abby never raised her eyes from the ground. She was always looking for money. When her friends met her and said, "Hi Abby! How are you?" Abby would look at them as if to say, "Don't bother me. Can't you see I'm busy looking for money?"

The older Abby became, the crabbier she became. That's why people started to call her Crabby Abby.

By the time Crabby Abby was seventy years old, she had found 12,000 pennies and 20,000 buttons. But by that time she was also an old crab who was always complaining about something or other.

For example, when she found another button she would say, "I don't like these new buttons. I don't like their colors. When I was a young girl, buttons were a lot prettier."

Have you ever met a Crabby Abby? There are lots of them. There are lots of people who are always complaining about something or other.

Of course, once you start looking for things to complain about, you can always find them, just as when you start looking for pennies and buttons you can always find them.

The Bible has something to say about Crabby Abbies. It says there shouldn't be any. It says there is no room for Crabby Abbies in God's world. It says people should rejoice in the Lord always. When people rejoice always, they no longer have time to complain.

44

Showdown

Gorillas and elephants and tigers are animals of the jungle. They fight a lot. When they fight, this is what they do. Gorillas beat their chests. Elephants blow their trunks. Tigers snarl.

Why do they? The answer is easy. They want the other animals they fight with to see what it is that makes them strong.

Gorillas beat their chests. They tell the other animals: See how strong our arms are! Our arms are so strong, we can hug you to death with them.

Elephants blow their trunks. They tell the other animals: See how strong our trunks are? We can grab you and throw you up into the air with them.

Tigers snarl and show their teeth. They tell the other animals: See how strong our teeth are? We can chew you to pieces with them.

Gorillas show their strong arms. Elephants show their strong trunks. Tigers show their strong teeth. What do you show when someone wants to fight you? Do you show your fists? Do you say, "Look how strong my fists are"? Do you say, "If you hit me with your fists, I'll hit you with mine"?

What does Jesus tell you to do? He tells you not to strike back when someone hits you. He tells you not to kick back when someone kicks you.

Why does Jesus tell you that? The answer is simple. He doesn't want you to behave like an animal in the jungle. He wants you to behave like one of his children.

Adapted with permission from *Father Ike's Stories for Children* (paper, 64 pp.), © 1988 by Isaias Powers, CP, published by Twenty-Third Publications, P.O. Box 180, Mystic, CT 06355.

45

Are You Afraid of God?

When I was about four years old, a woman who was nine feet tall lived across the street from our house. Well, not really. It only seemed that she was nine feet tall.

This nine-foot-tall woman had a booming voice. When she spoke, everybody in the street could hear her. When she laughed, all the windows of the houses on our street rattled. And when she shouted, all the trees on our street trembled and dropped some of their leaves.

I was deathly afraid of this woman. When I saw her walking down the street, I always crossed over to the other side. Just to be on the safe side.

So you can well imagine how upset I was when my mother told me that the next day she had to go away and that I had to stay with that big woman across the street. "Oh, no!" I thought, "Not with her!"

The next morning when my mother dropped me off my heart was pounding. I was scared. I wondered, "Will I come out of this alive?"

But after my mother left, this woman asked me, "Johnny, would you like a cookie?"

"Yes, ma'am," I squeaked.

After I finished it, she said, "Perhaps you would like another one?"

"Yes, ma'am," I answered. This time my voice was not so squeaky.

Then she read me a story. And after that still another story. So by the time my mom came to get me the big woman and little me were the best of friends.

Children sometimes think of God the way I first thought of the woman on our street. They think God is a big giant with a booming voice. They think God is someone to be afraid of.

If you think that way, if you think God is a big giant in the sky with a booming voice, then listen to what Jesus says about God. God is exactly like me, Jesus says. When you see me, you've seen God, for the two of us are the same.

Are you afraid of Jesus? Of course not. Then why be afraid of God?

46

This Is My Father's World

A couple of years ago I spent two weeks in Switzerland. Switzerland is known for its beautiful mountains. From my hotel room I could see some of these mountains.

One afternoon as I was enjoying the beautiful view while sitting on the small balcony of my hotel room, a scary thought came to me.

I thought: What if? What if all these mountains aren't part of God's world at all? What if this whole world isn't God's world at all? What if the whole world is actually the head of a big giant?

What if the grass the cows are eating on the mountain slopes isn't grass at all, but hair—hair growing out of the head of a big giant?

What if those cows aren't cows at all but lice living on the head of this big giant?

What if the mountains I'm looking at aren't mountains at all, but bumps on the head of this giant?

What if some stars had fallen on this giant's head so that now he has big bumps on it—bumps that are hurting badly?

And what if suddenly a giant hand would appear out of nowhere and start rubbing those bumps?

And what if, by rubbing those bumps, those hands would kill those cows and smash the hotel I am in and kill everybody inside?

What if, I thought.

But then I thought: That cannot be, for this is my Father's world. I am not living on a giant's head. I am living in a world that God made.

> *This is my Father's world:*
> *Why should my heart be sad?*
> *The Lord is King, let the heavens ring!*
> *God reigns: let the earth be glad.*

47

Just Wondering

Do you ever sit down and wonder about why things are the way they are? For example, do you ever wonder why you have only two eyes. Why don't you have three eyes, two eyes in front and a third eye in the back of your head so that you can keep an eye on what people are doing behind your back?

Do you ever wonder why you have two ears and only one mouth? Why don't you have two mouths and one ear? Is it because God wants you to listen more and speak less?

Do you ever wonder why spiders can walk up the wall and across the ceiling upside down? Don't you ever wish God had made you in such a way that you could do the same?

Do you ever wonder why, when you get bored, you become ornery and hard to live with? "Johnny, stop pestering your little sister!" your mom will say. "What's the matter with you? Are you bored or something?" she will ask. And you answer, "Yes, I'm bored. I don't know what to do."

But when a dog gets bored, what does it do? It goes to sleep. Now, why didn't God make you like a dog? Every time you got bored you would go to sleep. It would make your mom a lot happier. It also would make your sister a lot happier.

And do you ever wonder why God made the sky blue and not green? "Yuk!" you say. "Imagine the sky being green! It would make me sick!"

But what if the sky were green and always had been green? Then you wouldn't know any better. Then if someone would ask, "Why isn't the sky blue?" you would say, "Are you crazy? What's wrong with the sky being green?"

Do you ever wonder about things like that? I was just wondering.

48

Do You Know the Shepherd?

Once upon a time two friends went to the same school. When they grew up they went to different cities. One became a pastor of a church. The other became an actor, a very famous actor. Sadly, however, he forgot all about Jesus.

Many years later, when the actor grew old, his friends honored him at a special dinner. To this dinner they invited the actor's old school friend, the one who became a pastor. He came and they all had a good time.

When the dinner was over one of the guests asked the actor to read a poem to them. "I will do that," the actor said, "only if my old school friend will read the same poem."

The actor stood up and read to them from memory the psalm that begins, "The Lord is my shepherd, I shall not want." When he was finished, all the guests stood up and clapped their hands.

Then it was the pastor's turn. He stood up, pulled an old Bible out of his pocket and read the same psalm. He did not read it from memory, he read if from the Bible, as he so often had done when he visited sick people.

When he was finished, nobody stood up, nobody clapped, and it was very quiet for a while. Then the actor stood up and said to the guests, "Do you know what the difference is between my friend and me? I know the psalm, but he knows the shepherd of the psalm."

49

The Evil King

Once upon a time lived an evil king. This king had only one wish. His one wish was to conquer all the countries in the world. It took a while, but finally he did. This made the evil king very proud. It made him so proud that he had statues of himself placed in all city parks and in all important buildings.

The evil king also wanted his statues placed in all the churches, but the ministers of these churches would not hear of it. They told the king, "You are great, but God is greater. In our churches we worship only the greatest. So we will not allow your statues to be placed in our churches."

The evil king then said, "If the ministers think that God is greater than I am, then I must conquer God." For seven years he had his workmen build big planes. With these planes he planned to fly to heaven to conquer God.

When at last the planes were ready, the evil king gathered his soldiers and said, "Let's go into the planes, fly to heaven, and conquer God."

But right then God sent many mosquitos. These mosquitos stung the king's hands and his face. This made the king so mad that he drew his sword and slashed the air. But all his slashing didn't kill a single mosquito.

Then the king shouted, "Get me a blanket so I can wrap it around me and be safe from mosquitos." But when he wrapped a blanket around him, one mosquito got inside it. This mosquito crept inside the king's ear and stung him. The sting burned like fire and the poison entered the king's brain. The king threw off the blanket and, screaming with pain, danced in front of his soldiers.

The soldiers laughed and said, "Look at our mighty king. He wanted to beat God. But one mosquito beat him."

Adapted from a fairy tale of Hans Christian Andersen.

50

Who Is God?

Once upon a time a little fish swam up to his mother and asked, "Mom, what is this water that I hear so much about?"

His mother laughed and said, "You silly little fish! Why, water is all around you. Without water you could not swim. Without water you would be dead. If you want to know what water is, swim to the top of the pond and stick your head above the water. Then you'll find out what water is."

Once upon a time there was a baby deer. One day she walked up to her mother and asked, "Mom, what is this air that I hear so much about?"

Her mother laughed and said, "You silly little deer! Why, air is all around you. Without air you could not breathe. Without air you would be dead. If you want to know what air is, stick your head under water. Then you'll find out what air is."

Once upon a time there was a little worm. One day he crawled up to his mother and asked, "Mom, what is this soil that I hear so much about?"

His mother laughed and said, "You silly little worm! Why, the soil is all around you. Without the soil you could not crawl. Without the soil you would be dead. If you want to know what soil is, stick your head above the ground. Then you'll find out what soil is."

Once upon a time there was a little girl. One day she walked up to her mother and asked, "Mom, who is this God that I hear so much about?"

Her mother laughed and said, "You silly little girl! Why, God is all around you. Without God you could not live. Without God you would be dead. God is to you what water is to the fish and what air is to the deer and what soil is to the worm."

Adapted from Paul J. Wharton, *Stories and Parables for Preachers and Teachers* (New York: Paulist Press, 1986), p. 14. Used by permission.

51

Walking on Water

Once upon a time a hunter's dog died. So the hunter went to a pet shop and told the owner, "I need a good hunting dog. Do you have one?"

"Yes, I do," the man said. "I have a very good hunting dog for you. She's a little expensive, but you won't be disappointed in her. I promise."

The hunter bought the dog and the next day took her hunting near a lake. After a while a flock of ducks flew overhead. He aimed his rifle, fired a shot, and hit one of them. The duck dropped in the middle of the lake.

"Go get it!" the hunter told his new dog. And what do you think the dog did? Instead of jumping into the water like all hunting dogs do, this dog walked on top of the water, grabbed the duck between her teeth, walked back across the water, and dropped the duck at her master's feet.

"I don't believe this! I don't believe this!" the hunter kept saying. "I must show this to my best friend." So he invited his best friend to go hunting with him the next day.

Again the hunter shot a duck, which dropped into the lake. Again he told his dog, "Go get it!" And again the dog walked on top of the water, grabbed the duck, walked back across the water, and dropped the duck at her master's feet.

The proud hunter turned to his friend and asked him, "Did you notice anything special about my dog?" "Yes," his friend said, "your dog doesn't know how to swim."

The hunter's friend missed the miracle. You and I do too. All the time. There are miracles all around us and we don't see them. For example, take the fact that we were born, that we are alive, that we are listening with our ears and thinking with our brains and breathing with our lungs and seeing with our eyes. All of these things are miracles! Don't you agree?

52

Pleasing People

Once upon a time a father and his son took a donkey to town to sell it. The father sat on the donkey and the boy walked next to it.

People saw it and said, "How terrible! The big man sits on the donkey and the little boy walks next to it! Shame on you, old man!"

"That's enough of that!" the father said. So he got off the donkey and said to his son, "You sit on the donkey. I will walk next to it."

People saw it and said, "How terrible! The young boy sits on the donkey and the old man walks next to it! Shame on you, young boy!"

"That's enough of that!" the boy said. So he said to his father, "We'll both ride on the donkey's back." Which they did.

People saw it and said, "How cruel! Two people sitting on the poor donkey!"

"That's enough of that!" the father and his son said. So they both got off and walked next to the donkey.

People saw it and said, "How crazy! The donkey is carrying nothing on its back and those two are walking next to it."

"That's enough of that!" the father and his son said. So they carried the donkey the rest of the way.

You can never please everyone, can you? Nor should you ever try. For no matter what you do, there will always be people who don't like what you do.

You must do what is right. You must do what pleases God.

53

Letting Go

Once upon a time a mountain climber was walking down a narrow mountain path, he stumbled, lost his balance, and began sliding down the mountain side.

Fortunately, he was able to grab hold of a small bush. Scared, the mountain climber called out, "Is anyone here? Is anyone here to help me? Please hurry!" To his great surprise a voice said, "Yes, I am here. I am God."

The mountain climber said, "Please, God, help me. I can't hold on to this bush much longer."

Then God said, "Before I help you, I want to ask you a question. Do you believe in me?"

The mountain climber answered, "Of course I believe in you. I go to church every Sunday. I pray every day. I read my Bible every day. Of every ten dollars I earn I give one dollar to the church."

Then God asked, "But do you really believe in me?" The mountain climber was getting more and more desperate. "Yes, God," he said, "I really do believe in you."

"In that case," God said, "why don't you let go of the bush and trust that I will catch you?" The mountain climber stammered, "But, God, if I let go of the bush. . . ."

Then God asked again, "If you really believe in me, why don't you let go of the bush?"

My question to you is: If you had been that mountain climber, would you have let go of the bush?

Adapted from Paul J. Wharton, *Stories and Parables for Preachers and Teachers* (New York: Paulist Press, 1986), p. 24. Used by permission.

54

God in You

Once upon a time, in a far-away country, travelers stopped at a farm where a young boy lived. They needed water. So they asked the boy, "Is it OK if we draw some water from your well?" The boy said, "Go right ahead!"

After the travelers had drawn enough water, they stood looking down into the well. This made the boy curious. So he asked them, "What are you looking at?"

The travelers said, "Don't you know who lives at the bottom of the well?" The boy said, "No, I don't. Tell me."

The travelers said, "God lives down there." The boy said, "Lift me up so I can see for myself."

The travelers lifted him up and the boy looked down at the water below. There he saw the reflection of his own face. "But that's me," he shouted. "That's not God; that's me."

Then one of the travelers said, "Now you know where God lives. God lives inside of you."

God lives in two places at once. God lives in heaven; but God also lives on earth. But where on earth does God live? In the television set? In the refrigerator? In the cookie jar? Where on earth does God live?

You know where? Inside of you. The Bible asks, "Don't you know that God's Spirit lives in you?" Not in the television set, not in the refrigerator, not in the cookie jar, but in you.

Next time you look at yourself in the mirror, say to yourself, "I'm looking at a place where God lives on earth."

55

Three Wise Guys

Three wise men of Gotham
Went to sea in a bowl:
If the bowl had been stronger
My song would have been longer.

You probably know this nursery rhyme. You have heard it many times. Why isn't the story longer? What happened to these three men? They probably drowned. Why? Because their bowl tipped over.

Going to sea in a bowl wasn't a smart thing to do. You don't need a lot of brains to figure that out. If you want my honest opinion, I don't think these were wise men. These were wise guys. These were wise guys who went around telling everyone, "Yes, we know what we are doing!" "Yes, that bowl is strong enough!" "Yes, it will hold the three of us!" "No, it won't tip over!"

Perhaps the nursery rhyme should read this way:

Three wise guys of Gotham
Went to sea in a bowl:
If they had been smart,
They would have said, "Let's not start!"

There is a big difference between a wise man and a wise guy. Do you know what the difference is?

Jesus says, "This is the difference. Wise guys build their houses on the sand. Soon the rain falls, the flood comes, the wind huffs and puffs and blows their houses down. Wise men build their houses on the rock. Wise men build their lives on Jesus. Soon the rain falls, the flood comes, the wind huffs and puffs, but their lives do not fall down."

My question to you is: Are you a wise "man" or a wise "guy"?

56

Salt or Sponges?

Once upon a time, so an old story goes, lived two donkeys. The name of one donkey was Hee Haw. The name of the other donkey was Haw Hee. Hee Haw carried a load of salt. Haw Hee carried a load of something else.

After walking for a couple of hours they came to a stream. "I'll walk through it first," Hee Haw said.

Now you know, of course, that when you put salt in water, it disappears. It dissolves.

After Hee Haw had crossed the stream, he called back to Haw Hee, "Something wonderful has happened to me. I've lost my load."

"Great!" Haw Hee said. "I want to lose my load too." Then she entered the stream and something terrible happened. She drowned. She drowned because she was carrying a load of sponges, and sponges do not dissolve in water. Sponges soak up water, so that Haw Hee's load became heavier and heavier, until at last it pulled her under water and she drowned.

Some people are like Hee Haw. Others are like Haw Hee. Peter, one of Jesus' followers, was like Hee Haw, the donkey who lost his load. Peter lied and said he did not know Jesus. Lying about Jesus made Peter feel sad. That was Peter's load.

But Peter got rid of his load. He gave it to God. When God forgave him, Peter's load dissolved.

Judas, another one of Jesus' followers, is like Haw Hee, the donkey who drowned. Judas sold Jesus for money. After he sold Jesus, he felt bad. That was Judas' load. But instead of giving his load to God, Judas kept it. When you do that, your load becomes heavier and heavier, until at last it drags you down.

When you do something bad, something that makes you feel sad, give it to God; ask God to forgive you. When you do, you will say like Hee Haw, "Something wonderful has happened to me. I've lost my load."

57

So Much To Learn!

When you grow up you go to school. Why? Because there is so much to learn. For example, there is so much to learn about cows. Listen to what a young boy in England said about a cow before he went to school.

"A cow has six sides: right, left, upper, below, front, and back. At the back is a tail on which hangs a brush. With this brush the cow sends the flies away so they do not fall into the milk. The head is to grow horns and so the mouth can be somewhere. The horns are to butt with and the mouth is to moo with. Under the cow hangs the milk. It is arranged for milking. When people milk the cow, the milk comes and there is never an end to the supply. The cow does not eat much, but what it eats, it eats twice so that it gets enough. When it is hungry it moos and when it says nothing it is because all of its insides are filled up with grass."

This boy had a lot to learn about cows.

When you grow up you also go to church school. Why? Because there is so much to learn about the Bible. Listen, for example, to this conversation between a young girl and her church school teacher. The teacher asked her, "How far is Dan from Beersheba?"

Now, Dan is the name of a city in the north of Israel and Beersheba is the name of a city in the south of Israel.

"How far is Dan from Beersheba?"

The little girl asked, "Teacher, do I understand that Dan and Beersheba are names of cities?"

"They are indeed," the teacher replied.

"That's news to me," the little girl said. "I always thought that Dan and Beersheba were husband and wife. You know . . . like Sodom and Gomorrah."

As I said, when you grow up you go to school because there is so much to learn. Do you agree?

58

Who Will Help?

Once upon a time a chicken named Scrawny lived on a farm. Scrawny was always scratching in the dirt.

One day, after scratching a lot, Scrawny found some grains of wheat. "Who will help me plant the wheat?" she called out. "Not I," said the cat. "Not I," said the dog. "Not I," said the duck.

"Very well then," Scrawny said, "I will have to do it all by myself."

When the wheat was tall and ripe, Scrawny called out, "Who will help me cut the wheat?" "Not I," said the cat. "Not I," said the dog. "Not I," said the duck.

"Very well then," said Scrawny, "I will have to do it all by myself."

After Scrawny had cut the wheat, she called out, "Who will help me thresh the wheat?" "Not I," said the cat. "Not I," said the dog. "Not I," said the duck.

"Very well then," Scrawny said, "I will have to do it all by myself."

After she had threshed the wheat, Scrawny called out, "Who will help me take the wheat to the mill to have it ground into flour?" "Not I," said the cat. "Not I," said the dog. "Not I," said the duck.

"Very well then," Scrawny said, "I will have to do it all by myself."

After the wheat had been ground into flour, Scrawny called out, "Who will help me make this flour into bread?" "Not I," said the cat. "Not I," said the dog. "Not I," said the duck.

"Very well then," Scrawny said, "I will have to do it all by myself."

After Scrawny had baked a delicious loaf of bread, she called

Adapted from the story "The Little Red Hen."

out, "Who will eat this bread?" "I will," said the cat. "I will," said the dog. "I will," said the duck. And they all came running to eat her delicious bread.

Does Scrawny remind you of someone? Doesn't she remind you of your mom? Every day your mom cooks a delicious meal for you. This keeps her very busy. So once in a while she will call out, "Who can help me a minute?" or "Who can empty the dishwasher for me?" "Not I," your brother will say. "Not I," your sister will say. "Not I," you will say as you quietly disappear.

But as soon as the meal is ready and your mother calls out, "Time to eat!" you all come running.

Now that just isn't fair, is it?

59

Fixing Up the Past

Once upon a time a man who lived a very sinful life woke up one morning and said to himself, "I can't go on living like this. I must fix up my life. If only I knew how. Maybe my pastor knows how. I'd better go see him."

So he visited his pastor and said, "Pastor, I have lived a very sinful life. I have sinned as many times as there are feathers on a chicken. What can I do to fix up my past?"

His pastor told him, "Go buy yourself a live chicken."

"Buy myself a live chicken?" the man asked, "Whatever for?"

"Do as I told you," his pastor said.

So the man bought a live chicken. Then he went back to his

Adapted from Paul J. Wharton, *Stories and Parables for Preachers and Teachers* (New York: Paulist Press, 1986), p. 46. Used by permission.

pastor and said, "I've done what you told me to do. Now what do I do?"

"What I want you to do next," the pastor said, "is take that live chicken and walk through the entire village with it. As you do, I want you to pull the feathers out of the chicken and place one feather at each front door."

The man did as he was told. He walked through the entire village, pulled the feathers out of the chicken as he went along, and placed one feather at each front door.

Then he went back to his pastor and said, "I have done what you told me to do. Now what do I do?"

The pastor said, "What I want you to do next is go back and collect all the feathers and stick them back into the chicken."

"But that's impossible," the man said. "The wind has blown them all away. And even if it hasn't, even if I could collect all the feathers, I could never stick them back into the chicken."

"Correct," the pastor said. "It simply is impossible. It is just as impossible for you to go back into your past and fix it up. There's only one Person who can do that."

Now my question to you is, Do you know who that Person is?

60

Oh, What a Relief It Is!

Once upon a time a rooster lived on an animal farm. Every morning this rooster made the sun rise. At least he thought he did. Every morning he would get up early, fly to the top of the barn roof, cocka-doodle-doo a few times, and then wait for the sun to rise above the horizon.

Every morning the animals on the ground below would thank the rooster. They would say things like, "Thanks for making the sun rise again!" Or, "Good job, Rooster! You did it again!"

Making the sun rise every morning was a big responsibility for the rooster. "What if I got sick?" the rooster often thought. "Or what if I died? Then who would make the sun rise? What if no one did? What if the sun would never rise again? Then the world would grow dark and cold. After a while, the grass and the trees would die. Then, after a while, every animal on the farm would die. So I'd better be on top of the barn roof every morning!" the rooster told himself again and again.

But one day the rooster overslept. The night before, he had been to a party and stayed too late. All the animals were waiting for the rooster to make the sun rise, but he never showed up.

But do you know what? Even though the rooster overslept, the sun came up anyway. This made the other animals mad—mad at the rooster. They told him, "All these years we believed that you make the sun rise. But you don't. Shame on you, Mr. Rooster! Shame on you!"

As you can well understand, the rooster felt terrible. All these years he too had believed that he made the sun rise, only to find out that he didn't.

But the rooster felt not only shame and disappointment. He also felt relief. "Oh, what a relief it is!" he kept singing to himself. "Oh, what a relief it is to know that I don't make the sun rise but that somebody else does."

61

Let's Kill It!

Once upon a time a little boy had a pet turtle. One day he came running into the house. He was all upset. "Mom," he cried, "my turtle just rolled over and died." He cried and cried.

After he had used up all his tears, his mother took him by the hand and walked to the place where the dead turtle lay. To make her little boy feel better, the mother said, "Do you know what we could do? We could have a funeral for your turtle. We could bury it in the tin box where we keep the candy. And after we bury it we can have a party, a funeral party. Wouldn't that be nice?"

By this time the little boy was smiling again. "Yes," he said, "that would be very, very nice."

"We'll have balloons," the mother said. "We'll have some friends over. We'll have a funeral cake and funeral ice cream."

When the little boy heard his mother promise all these good things, he grinned from ear to ear. He could hardly wait for the funeral to be over and for the party to begin.

But then, suddenly, the turtle rolled back on its legs and slowly moved away. The little boy looked startled, then disappointed. With the turtle alive again, of course, there would be no party. The boy even became angry. "How dare the turtle spoil my party!" Pointing to the turtle he said, "Oh, Mom, let's kill it!"

I'm sure you would like to know where this little boy lives and what his name is. Well, I've got some bad news for you. He lives at your house and he has your name. For each time you are selfish and don't care about what happens to others, you act just like that little boy.

Adapted with permission from *Storytelling: Imagination and Faith* (paper, 232 pages), © 1984 by William J. Bausch, published by Twenty-Third Publications, P.O. Box 180, Mystic, CT 06355.

62

Being Angry

Have you ever been angry? I mean really angry? So angry that your face turned red and you screamed and stamped your foot? If you have, then the story I am about to tell is for you.

Once upon a time lived a little girl whose name was Angela, which means angel. But there was nothing angelic about her. She got angry very quickly. Each time she didn't get her way she would go out of control.

One day Angela got so angry and stamped her foot so hard, that it went straight through the floor of her upstairs bedroom and through the ceiling of the living room.

No matter how hard she tried, Angela could not free her leg. Nor could her mom or dad. They pulled and pulled, but it was no use. The leg did not move an inch.

"I have an idea," Angela's father said. "I'll pour a can of engine oil down her leg to make it slippery. That should do it!"

But it didn't. All the oil did was run down Angela's leg and drip on the new living room carpet, which upset Angela's mother very much.

"I'd better call the police," Angela's father said. Maybe they know what to do. So a policeman came and looked at Angela's leg. "I know just what to do," he said. "We'll make a hole in the ceiling of Angela's room. Then we'll make a hole in the roof. Then we'll let down a rope from a helicopter, tie it around Angela's waist, and pull her out."

So they knocked a hole in the ceiling and in the roof, let down a rope from a helicopter, and tied it around Angela's waist. But when the helicopter tried to pull her out, it pulled up the whole house. Angela's leg just would not move.

Adapted from Kenneth B. Welles, *Children's Sermons* (Philadelphia: West-minster), pp. 37–38. Copyright © 1954, 1982. By permission of Thomas Welles Barber.

Then, after nothing had worked, Angela's parents decided to call the minister. The minister looked at Angela's leg and said, "Do you know what the Bible says about stamping your foot? It says that stupid people express their anger openly, by stamping their feet, but that wise people control their anger."

I forgot what happened next. All I remember is that Angela somehow got her leg out and that she never stamped her foot again.

63

Mr. Puffer

You reap whatever you sow. You harvest whatever you plant. If you sow tomatoes, you reap tomatoes. If you sow strawberries, you reap strawberries.

You reap whatever you sow. That's a law of nature. That's a law God made. That's a law no one in the whole wide world can change.

When you sow kindness, you reap kindness. When you sow unkindness, you reap unkindness. When you hit your brother, chances are your brother hits you back.

You reap whatever you sow. Some people think they can fool that law. They think they can sow unkindness and reap kindness. But it does not work that way. Which reminds me of a story.

Once upon a time lived a crabby man whose name was Puffer. Even though Mr. Puffer had a candy store, nothing about him

Adapted from Kenneth B. Welles, *Children's Sermons* (Philadelphia: Westminster), pp. 83–84. Copyright © 1954, 1982. By permission of Thomas Welles Barber.

was sweet. He was a sourpuss. He never laughed. He never smiled. He never spoke a kind word.

One night Mr. Puffer reaped what he had sown. The telephone rang. Mr. Puffer picked up the telephone and in an unkind voice said, "Hello."

"Is this Puffer's?" a voice asked.

"Yes, this is Puffer's," Mr. Puffer answered.

"Is this Puffer and Company?" the voice asked.

"Yes, this is Puffer and Company," Mr. Puffer answered.

"I want to talk to Mr. Puffer," the voice said.

"This is Mr. Puffer," Mr. Puffer said.

"Mr. John Puffer?" the voice asked.

"Yes, Mr. John Puffer," Mr. Puffer said.

"Mr. John Ronald Puffer?" the voice asked.

By this time Mr. Puffer was so mad that he shouted into the telephone, "Yes, Mr. John Ronald Puffer. Now what is it you want?"

The voice said, "Well, puff away, old Puffer!"

It is as the Bible says, "You reap whatever you sow."

64

With Laughter and Tears

Once upon a time, so an old story goes, two brothers lived side by side. One was married and had seven children. The other was not married. These two brothers shared a farm. Because both brothers worked hard and the soil was good and the weather was right, the harvests were rich.

Each year the brothers would divide the harvest evenly. Each would get one half of the grain and store it in a separate barn.

One night the unmarried brother could not go to sleep. He kept thinking about his married brother and his seven children. He told himself, "It just isn't right that each of us should get half of the grain. My brother has a big family and needs the grain more than I do."

So each night the unmarried brother took some of the grain stored in his barn and secretly carried it to his brother's barn.

That same night the married brother too could not sleep. He kept thinking about his unmarried brother. He told himself, "It just isn't right that each of us should get half of the grain. I have seven children. When I grow old they will look after me. My brother is all by himself. When he grows old he has no one to look after him. Surely he needs more grain now to save for later."

So each night the married brother took some of the grain stored in his barn and secretly carried it to his brother's barn.

Each night the two brothers would give away some of their grain, and each morning they would find that they still had the same amount of grain as before. And they would wonder how this could be possible.

One night the two brothers met each other halfway between the barns. At once they realized what had been happening. Then they hugged each other with laughter and tears.

Adapted from a Jewish folk story.

65

Grace

Grace. You must have heard that word at least a hundred times. But what is it? That's not easy to explain. So let me tell you a story that explains how grace works. These events took place many years ago when our country went through hard times and when many people were out of work.

One rainy night in New York City, a hungry old man was caught stealing a loaf of bread. He was arrested and sent to the judge. Now it so happened that the judge that night was Fiorello La Guardia. Fiorello La Guardia was the mayor of New York. Sometimes he would serve as judge, just to find out what was going on in his city.

When Mr. La Guardia heard that the old man had stolen a loaf of bread, he fined him ten dollars. "I am sorry," he said, "but the law is the law. When you break the law you deserve to be punished."

But then Mr. La Guardia took a ten dollar bill out of his wallet and told the old man that he would pay his fine for him.

After Mr. La Guardia had paid the ten dollar fine, he turned to the other people in the courtroom and fined each one of them fifty cents for living in a city that did not feed its hungry people. Then he passed his hat to collect all the fifty-cent fines and gave the old man the money that was in the hat, which was almost fifty dollars. He told the old man that he was free to go, and the old man left the courtroom with tears in his eyes because of the grace that Mr. La Guardia had shown him.

Grace is standing before the judge and the judge saying to you, "You have broken the law. And the law is the law. When you break it, you deserve to be punished. But—you don't have to pay the fine. I will pay the fine for you."

Adapted from Edward Chinn, *The Wonder of Words* (Lima, Ohio: C. S. S. Publishing, 1985). Use by permission.

66

Treasure in Heaven

Once upon a time lived an old married couple. The older they became, the more they worried about the future. They often asked, "What if we run out of money? Then who will take care of us? Who will pay our rent? Who will buy our food?"

Even though each day they prayed, "Give us this day our daily bread," and even though God answered their prayer each day, they still worried about the future.

One morning, when the woman walked into the kitchen, she found a large jewel lying on top of the stove. She hurried to her husband and said, "Look what I found! A large jewel!" The husband looked at it and exclaimed, "Now we don't have to worry about the future any more, for this jewel is worth a lot of money. We can sell it and have plenty of everything."

That night the woman had a dream. She dreamed that she was in heaven and that an angel showed her all around. The angel showed her a place where many beautiful chairs were placed. Each chair had a beautiful jewel in it. The angel explained, "These chairs are for people who trust in God and not in money." The angel also showed the woman the chair that was waiting for her. "When you come to heaven," the angel said, "this will be your chair."

When the woman looked closely at her chair, she saw an empty spot for a large jewel. She asked the angel, "What happened to the jewel?" The angel replied, "The missing jewel is the one you found on your stove. You received it ahead of time. If you sell it and spend the money, it cannot be put back again."

This is what the woman dreamed. In the morning she told her husband about her dream. For a long time they talked about what

Adapted from Søren Kierkegaard, *Attack Upon Christendom*, copyright © 1944 by Princeton University Press. Reprinted by permission of Princeton University Press.

to do with the jewel. They decided to return it, for, they said, "We must trust in God and not in the jewel."

That evening, before going to bed, they laid the jewel on the stove and prayed that God would take it back. And God did. The next morning, when the couple looked at the stove, they found that the jewel was gone.

The old couple felt happy. They knew that it is better to have a treasure in heaven, where it cannot be stolen, than to have it on earth.

67

Conscience

Once upon a time lived a little girl who had a bad cold. All day long she went "Sniff, sniff."

Sitting on the tip of her nose was a tiny little man. And this tiny little man said to her, "Please don't sniff. Every time you sniff I lose my balance. I would appreciate it if you used your handkerchief."

The little girl was surprised to see that tiny man. She had never suspected there was anything on the tip of her nose.

"If I use my handkerchief," the girl said, "I might wipe you right off my nose, and I don't think that's what you want me to do. But what are you doing on the tip of my nose anyway?"

The tiny little man said, "My job is to show you what to do and what not to do. God told me to tell you that, so you better do as I say."

"But I thought my conscience told me that," the little girl

Adapted from Kenneth B. Welles, *Children's Stories* (Philadelphia: Westminster), pp. 46–47. Copyright © 1954, 1982. By permission of Thomas Welles Barber.

said. "I thought my conscience told me what to do and what not to do. And I thought my conscience was inside me."

"So it is! So it is!" the tiny little man said. "Your conscience is inside you. I am your conscience, and I live inside you."

"Then what are you doing on the tip of my nose?" the girl asked. The tiny little man answered, "Every once in a while it gets so stuffy inside that I have to come out to catch some fresh air. And what better place is there than the tip of your nose? But believe me, I am your conscience. God put me inside you. When I speak you'd better listen."

"I will," the little girl said. And she looked at the tip of her nose. "Well," she said, "what do you know! There really is someone sitting there."

If you don't believe my story, look at the tip of your own nose and see for yourself. There is someone there, isn't there? And if there isn't, then your conscience must have gone inside, where it belongs.

68

Plain Bottles

Once upon a time lived a man who was very wise. He was by far the wisest man in all the land. He was so wise that the king often invited him to the palace to ask for advice.

Though this man was wise, he was far from handsome. In fact, he was rather ugly. It was only after you listened to his wisdom that you forgot to notice how ugly he was.

Everybody in the palace liked him. Well, almost everybody, for the king's youngest daughter didn't like him one little bit. When the king asked her, "Why don't you like the wise man?" she answered, "Because he is so ugly!"

One day the king's youngest daughter met the ugly wise man in the hallway of the palace. She said to him, "My father tells me you are the wisest man in the land. If you are so wise, please tell me why God put so much wisdom in such an ugly man like you?"

The wise man was silent for a moment and then said, "Tell me, does your father have any wine?" "Of course, he does," the princess answered. "He has an entire room full of wine—the finest wine in the land."

"Where does your father keep the wine?" the wise man asked. "In large clay bottles," the princess answered.

"In clay bottles?" the wise man asked. "But don't you know that even the poorest farmer stores his wine in clay bottles? Wouldn't you expect your father to store his wine in bottles made of silver?" Then the wise man bowed and left.

Quickly the princess went to the wine room and told the wine keeper to pour all the wine out of the clay bottles and into silver bottles.

Soon after there was a big party in the palace. But as the guests tasted the wine, they put up their noses. The wine was sour and tasted like vinegar.

When the king was told that all his wine had turned sour

because his youngest daughter had told the wine keeper to pour it into silver bottles, he called his daughter and scolded her for having spoiled all his wine.

After the party was over the princess raced to the wise man's room. She shouted, "Why did you trick me into pouring the wine from clay bottles into silver bottles?"

"I am truly sorry this happened," the wise man said, "but perhaps now you can understand why God put so much of his wisdom in plain people like me. Wisdom, like wine, is best kept in plain bottles."

69

What Is God Like?

What is God like? If you want to know, listen to this story.

Once upon a time lived an Indian boy whose name was Red Feather. Soon he would be sixteen years old. Then he would no longer be a boy but become a man. He could hardly wait.

But first he had to pass some tests. He had to show that he could run fast, hunt well, and fight well. The most difficult test, however, came at the very end.

One dark night, when the stars didn't shine, his father asked, "Red Feather, are you ready for the last test?" "I am," Red Feather answered. "Then follow me," his father said.

They walked into the forest, and then they walked deeper and deeper into the forest until they came to a clearing. "To prove that you have courage," the father said to Red Feather, "you must stay here all night. You must stay here until I come for you in the morning." Then he walked off.

At first Red Feather was not afraid. But then he began to hear

Adapted from a forgotten source.

some scary noises. The screeching of an owl. The howling of a wolf. Noises that gave him goose bumps.

After a while, Red Feather thought he saw things. Things that moved. Things that looked like dangerous animals. Suddenly he became afraid. He felt like running home. But then he remembered that this was his last test. So he stayed.

At last came dawn. Slowly it became lighter and lighter. Then all of a sudden his father stepped from behind a nearby tree. "Am I glad to see you!" Red Feather said. "Being out here alone was scary!" "But son," his father said, "you were never alone. I've been here all night with you, keeping an eye on you from behind this tree!"

What is God like? God is like that Indian father. At night sometimes, when you're all alone in the dark, when you feel afraid, when you hear scary noises or think you see scary things, you wish someone would be in the room with you.

Well, someone is. God always is. Keeping an eye on you.

70

A "Gotcha" Story

I once read a story that teaches you how to think. Are you ready? Do you know what a chimney sweep is? A chimney sweep is a person who climbs up on your roof and sweeps all the dirty soot out of your chimney. Once upon a time two chimney sweeps were busy cleaning out a big chimney. At one point they bent over just a little too far, and down the chimney they went. With a bang they landed in the fireplace below. The face of the one was clean; the face of the other was dirty.

My question is this: Which one of them goes to wash his face? The chimney sweep with the dirty face? Wrong! For he looks at the chimney sweep with the clean face and thinks, "My face must be just as clean." But the chimney sweep with the clean face looks at the one with the dirty face and thinks, "My face must be just as dirty." So he goes to wash his face.

The next day the same thing happens. Both chimney sweeps fall down the chimney again. The face of the one is dirty; the face of the other is clean.

My question is: Which one goes to wash his face this time? The chimney sweep with the clean face? Wrong! Because the day before, when he looked in the bathroom mirror, he noticed that his face wasn't dirty at all. And the chimney sweep with the dirty face noticed, when he looked in the mirror, that his face was dirty. So this time the chimney sweep with the dirty face goes to wash his face.

The next day the same thing happens again. Both fall down the chimney. The face of the one is dirty; the face of the other is clean.

My question is: Which one goes to wash his face? The one with the dirty face? Wrong! This time both chimney sweeps go to wash their faces. For didn't I tell you at the beginning that I was going to tell you a story that teaches you how to think? Well, now, let's do just that. Let's think.

Is it possible for two chimney sweeps to go down the same dirty chimney at the same time and for one of them to get his face dirty and for the other to keep his face clean? Of course not!

So it's a tricky story, isn't it? Each time you think you know the answer, it turns out that you are wrong. The answer is always different from what you expect it to be.

Jesus told lots of stories like that. They are called parables. And a parable is like a chimney. You read it, lean over just a little bit too far, and down you go. Ending up with a dirty face.

71

Humpty Dumpty

Humpty Dumpty sat on a tuffet
Right next to Miss Muffet.
There came a big spider
Who sat down beside her
And frightened Humpty Dumpty away.

"Wait a minute!" you say. "That's not right. Humpty Dumpty and Miss Muffet have nothing to do with each other. They don't belong in the same nursery rhyme. Each needs its own nursery rhyme. When you let Humpty Dumpty and Miss Muffet live in the same nursery rhyme, things don't make sense anymore.

You are right, of course. So let us send Miss Muffet away. Let's make sure that Humpty Dumpty lives in a nursery rhyme all by himself.

Humpty Dumpty sat on a wall,
Humpty Dumpty had a great fall;
All the king's horses
And all the king's men
Couldn't put Humpty Dumpty together again.

"That," you say, "is much better. Now the Humpty Dumpty nursery rhyme makes sense again."

But does it? Does it really make sense? Let me ask you a simple question: Who is Humpty Dumpty? Give up? See what I mean? It's not so easy as you thought.

Humpty Dumpty is you. Humpty Dumpty is me. Humpty Dumpty is all of us. Long, long ago, God made Humpty Dumpty. God looked at Humpty Dumpty and said, "That's the way I want Humpty Dumpty to be."

Then something terrible happened. Humpty Dumpty had a great fall. And ever since, things have not been going well with Humpty Dumpty. Ever since, Humpty Dumpty has been lying and stealing and fighting.

Now the big question is: Who can put Humpty Dumpty together again? All the king's horses can't do it. All the king's men can't do it. Who can do it?

The only one who can do it is God. And God is doing it. He is putting us together again. So now I wonder: When God is all through putting us together, what will we look like?

That is one of the many surprises God has for us.

72

Why Your Toes Are Short

What I want you to do is to look at your toes. Take off your shoes and socks and look at your toes a while. Does something strike you? Does a thought strike you that has never struck you before?

"Yes," you may say, "something does strike me. It strikes me how short my toes are. It strikes me that my toes are about half as long as my fingers."

Why do you think that is? Why would your toes be half as long as your fingers? Suppose your toes were as long as your fingers. Or suppose that your toes were even longer than that. Suppose they were as long as your arm. Then what?

Then you would need new shoes. Long shoes. Shoes longer than your arm. Then you would be stepping on a lot of people's toes. Then people would constantly be saying to you, "Hey, watch where you are going! You are stepping on my toes!" And then you would always be saying, "Oh, I'm sorry. I did not mean to step on your toes." And as you stepped off that person's toes you would be stepping on another person's toes again, for there would be long toes wherever you stepped.

When I was young we would sometimes say, "When you talk to Harry, don't step on his toes because they are very long." We did not mean to say that Harry actually had long toes so that he had to wear shoes longer than his arm. What we meant was that Harry's feelings were easily hurt so that you had to be careful what you said to him.

Look at your toes again. Why did God make them so short? God made our toes short so that we might not easily step on other people's toes and so that other people might not easily step on our toes. God made our toes short so that our feelings might not be easily hurt and so that we might not carelessly hurt others' feelings. Does that make sense?

73

Give Secretly

Once upon a time, in a faraway village, lived a man who had lots of money. But he never gave any of it to people who were poor. When beggars came to his door he would say, "Sorry, but I don't give money to beggars."

In that same village also lived a shoemaker. He did just the opposite of the rich man. He gave money to every beggar who came to his door.

One day the rich man died. Because he had been so stingy with his money, no one felt sad about his death and no one went to his funeral.

A few weeks after the rich man had died, some bad news went around the village. "Have you heard the latest?" someone would ask. "No, tell me!" someone else would say. "Well, the shoemaker no longer gives money to beggars." "He doesn't? Has he become just as stingy as the rich man who just died?"

The minister of the village church also heard the bad news. But rather than talk about it to others, he decided to talk to the shoemaker himself. He paid him a visit and asked him point blank: "Is it true what people are saying about you? Is it true that you have stopped giving money to beggars and poor people?"

The shoemaker answered the minister by telling this story. "Many, many years ago," the shoemaker told the minister, "the rich man who just died came to me with a bag full of money. He said to me, 'I want you to give this money to beggars and to the poor. But don't tell anyone whose money it is. Don't tell anyone that it is my money. Don't tell them until after I am dead.'

"After that visit," the shoemaker told the minister, "the rich man visited me once a month and gave me more money to give away. Even though I never gave away a penny of my own, I came to be known as the most generous person in the village."

The next Sunday, the minister told the people of his church what the shoemaker had told him. The rich man, he told the people, did what Jesus wants all of us to do. Jesus said, "When you give money to someone who needs it badly, don't let anyone know about it. Instead, give secretly. When you do, people will not praise you. They will praise God."

74

The Biggest Word

Once upon a time lived a mouse that was so smart her brothers and sisters called her Bighead. Bighead never played "hide and squeak" with them. She thought she was too smart for that.

Bighead and her family lived beneath the floor of a school. This was just the right place for her. All day long she could listen to what the teachers taught the children. She learned many big words and with these big words she tried to impress her brothers and sisters.

One night after supper Bighead said, "Do you know what big words I learned today? I learned the words a-rith-me-tic and ge-o-gra-phy and e-co-no-my. . . ."

Now it so happened that Bighead was standing beneath a hole in the floor. As she was bragging about all the big words she had learned, the paw of a cat suddenly reached down through that hole and grabbed her. SWOOP! Suddenly Bighead was gone.

"Bighead has been taken up to heaven!" her mother said. "Nonsense!" her father said, "The cat got her and ate her."

Everyone felt sorry for Bighead. But after about an hour, Bighead suddenly showed up again. "What happened?" they all

Adapted from "A Lesson for Bighead' in *Parables for Little People* by Lawrence Castagnola, S.J. Copyright © 1982 by Resource Publications, Inc., 160 East Virginia Street, No. 290, San Jose, CA 95112.

asked. "The cat almost ate me," Bighead said. "But when he was just about to eat me, I used one of my big words. I told him that if he ate me, he would get in-di-ges-tion. Then the cat asked me, 'In-di-ges-tion? What is that?' So I told him everything I know about how the stomach works. When he heard that he let me go."

"We're sure glad you're back," one of her brothers said. "So am I," said Bighead. "I thought I would never see you again. Now I know that there are much more important things than big words. Now I know that brothers and sisters and the little word *love* are the biggest things in the world."

Then Bighead asked, "Anyone want to play 'hide and squeak'?"

75

Are You Unhappy?

Once upon a time lived a man who was very unhappy. He was unhappy because the people around him were always stealing and lying and fighting. One day he told his family and friends, "I am leaving. I'm going to a city where people do none of these things. I'm going to a place where people are honest and help each other and treat each other with respect. I'm going to a city where earth and heaven meet."

He packed some food, kissed his family good-bye, and started walking. He walked all day. Just before the sun went down and the world turned dark, he found a place to sleep, just off the road. He ate some food and said his evening prayer. Then, before lying down to sleep, he placed his shoes in the middle of the road, making sure that they pointed in the direction he had been walking all day.

That night, while he was sleeping, a man came walking down that road. He saw those shoes and thought, "Hmmm, the man sleeping there pointed his shoes in the direction in which he will be traveling tomorrow. I'll play a trick on him. I'll turn his shoes around. I'll point them in the direction from which he came." And he did.

The next morning the traveler rose, said his morning prayer, ate some food, and started to walk in the direction in which his shoes were pointing, which, of course, was the direction of his hometown.

He walked all day, and just before the sun went down and the world turned dark, he thought he saw the city where earth and heaven meet.

It wasn't so large as he had expected. And it looked strangely familiar. He walked down a street that looked very much like the street he had lived on his whole life. He knocked at a door that looked very much like his own. He was greeted by a family that looked very much like his own. And he lived happily ever after in his own city, on his own street, in his own house, and with his own family.

What does this story mean? It means something very simple and very important. It means that the place to be happy is not in a far-away city with people you have never met, but in your own city with your own family. If you can't be happy there, you can't be happy anywhere.

76

Remember Who You Are

Once upon a time lived a little tiger. When this little tiger was still a baby she lost her family. "I must find my family," she kept saying to herself. Finally, after walking a very long time, she saw a flock of sheep. "This must be my family," she said. And she joined the sheep.

The little tiger copied everything the sheep did. When the sheep ate grass so did she. Even though she didn't like her first few bites of grass, she kept eating it. After a few days of trying, she ate grass as well as the sheep did.

The little tiger also learned to say "baa" like the other sheep. At first her "baa" didn't sound quite right, but after a few days her "baa" sounded just like the "baa" of the sheep.

At first it bothered the little tiger that her fur did not grow so long and woolly as that of the sheep. But the sheep were too busy eating grass even to notice. So she stopped worrying about her fur. "If no one cares what my fur looks like, why should I?" she asked herself.

Then, one day when the sheep were eating grass in the meadow, a loud roar came out of the nearby jungle. Soon a giant

A tale that probably originated in India and exists in many versions.

tiger appeared. The sheep started running as fast as they could. But something inside the little tiger told her not to run. Somehow she liked the sound of that roar and was not afraid of that big tiger.

The big tiger asked the little tiger, "Who are you?" "I'm a sheep," the little tiger answered. "You are not a sheep," the big tiger said, "you are a tiger." "I am?" the little tiger asked. "Of course, you are," the big tiger said. "Come over here and look at yourself in this pool of water."

Then, for the first time in her life, the little tiger saw herself. "Wow!" she said, "I look just like you." "Exactly," the big tiger said. "You look just like me because you are just like me. You are not a sheep; you are a tiger. You were born, not to say 'baa,' but to roar like me." And the big tiger threw back his head and roared.

When the little tiger heard that roar she suddenly knew who she was. "I am a tiger," she said. And she threw back her head and roared.

Now, I have a question to ask. Who, do you think, is that little tiger? That little tiger is you or me. Sometimes we forget who we really are. Sometimes we forget that we are followers of Jesus. Sometimes we use bad language or tell lies or say mean things about others.

Then, when our mom or dad reads stories about Jesus to us, we remember again who we really are. We remember that we are followers of Jesus. Because we are, we should talk like Jesus.

77

Birds Flying South

When it is fall and the weather turns cold and you look up at the sky long enough, you see many birds flying south. Birds do this every year. Every year they fly south in the fall and then fly north again in the spring.

In North America alone, every fall some ten billion birds fly south for the winter. Ten billion birds! Doesn't that make you wonder: How do these ten billion birds know when it is time to fly south? How do they know which way to fly? Who tells them? Who tells them when to fly? Who tells them which way to fly? How do these birds know when they have arrived? Why do these birds each year fly to the same area, sometimes even to the same tree?

We don't know very much about birds flying south. One thing we do know is that they always keep an eye on the sun. When birds build nests and look for food and raise their little birds, they always keep an eye on the sun. As soon as the days begin to grow shorter and the birds don't see so much of the sun anymore, something in their little heads tells them to get ready to fly south. Their bodies begin to store fat, for fat is energy, and energy is what they need to fly such a long way. Some birds fly two or three thousand miles without stopping once! Flying at fifty miles an hour, some birds fly for five days without taking a break, without eating, without sleeping!

Most birds are not in such a hurry. They take their time about it. They fly six to eight hours at a time. Then they stop to rest and eat and sleep.

Isn't that a miracle? Each year in North America ten billion birds fly south, knowing just when to leave, knowing just which way to fly, knowing just when they have arrived.

Who but God can make birds do that?

78

Who Has Seen God?

Snow is funny stuff, isn't it? What is snow made of? Of cotton? Of sugar candy? No, snow is made of water. Snow, really, is nothing but water frozen in the air.

Let's do some pretending. Pretend you go to Africa. Pretend you go to a country in Africa where it never snows, where the weather is always hot. Pretend you tell the children there: "In my country in certain months of the year we take water into our hands and make it into a round ball. In my country in certain months of the year we build forts out of water. In my country in certain months of the year we roll water into huge balls and make them look like people, with arms, a head, a nose, two ears, and a mouth."

Would those children believe you? They certainly would not. They would say to you, "You're crazy! You can't do things like that with water! You can't roll water into a ball! You can't build forts out of water!"

Why would they say that? They would say that because they have never *seen* snow.

Now you understand why so many people didn't believe what Jesus said. Because Jesus said, "I have seen God. I know what God is like. God is love. God loves you so much that he sent me to die for your sins."

When Jesus said that, the people laughed. They said, "You are crazy! God is not like that. God would never do a thing like that. God did not send you to die for us."

Just as you know what snow is like because you have *seen* snow, so Jesus knows what God is like because he has *seen* God. So you would be crazy if you didn't listen to what Jesus tells you about God.

79

An Odd Bird

We have an odd bird in our neighborhood. Last week he sat half-way up the TV antenna on our neighbor's roof, singing his heart out at five o'clock in the morning. So I told him, "Don't do this to me! Much as I like you, I like sleep even more."

I don't think the bird understood what I said, for at five o'clock the next morning he was doing it again.

I have done some thinking about this bird: "Maybe this is nothing unusual for this kind of bird. Maybe all his friends and brothers and sisters and uncles and aunts are doing the same thing." But then I thought, "If that is true, why aren't they up there with him? Why aren't they sitting half-way up that TV antenna at five o'clock in the morning, singing along with him?"

So I did some more thinking: "Maybe this bird has a problem. Maybe this bird is a problem. Maybe this bird is a big problem to his family and they have kicked him out of the nest. Maybe they told him, 'You're too much for us! Get lost!'"

But then I did some more thinking. "Maybe this bird is a preacher. Maybe he went to Bird Seminary. Maybe he just became a minister of a neighborhood bird church. Maybe the TV antenna is his pulpit. Maybe his singing is really his preaching."

Well, who knows? One thing I do know: It's an odd bird. But then, God made so many odd birds. Because he did, this world is such an interesting place. And because it is, there should never be a dull moment in your life. If there is, don't blame God. Blame yourself.

80

Mud Puddles

What are little girls made of? Sugar and spice and everything nice. That's what little girls are made of. And what are little boys made of? Snakes and snails and puppy dog tails. That's what little boys are made of.

But do little girls and little boys know what mud puddles are made of? "Yes, we do," you say. "Mud puddles are made of water and dirt." Which is true, but there is more. For mixed in with the water and dirt are thousands of little creatures.

As, for example, the little creature called the amoeba. Amoebas are so tiny you can't even see them. They don't have mouths, yet they can eat. When they get hungry, they wrap themselves around other little creatures and eat them. "Hi there," they will say. "My name is Amoeba. What's yours? Do you mind if I get friendly with you and wrap myself around you?" Gobble, gobble.

Another little creature moving around in mud puddles is the paramecium. A paramecium has no arms and no legs, yet it is able to move around. It looks like a tiny hairy slipper. The hair helps it to move around.

Sometimes other little creatures will attack a paramecium. When they do, the paramecium knows just what to do. It shoots tiny darts with poisoned tips at those creatures.

Amazing, isn't it, that all these things are going on in a mud puddle? Amazing, isn't it, that God made these tiny creatures in such a way that they can live in a mud puddle? Now, if God cares about these creatures so tiny that you can't even see them, don't you think he cares even more about you?

Inspired by a tract published by the Back to God Tract Committee of the Christian Reformed Church, Grand Rapids, Michigan.

81

Little Puppy

Once upon a time a cute little puppy took a walk around her master's farm. When she met the horse, the horse said, "You must be new here. Well, little puppy, just remember: the farmer loves me more than any of the other animals. Do you know why? Because I pull all the heavy loads for him. Since you don't pull any loads for him, you are of no use to him."

Well, you can imagine how this made the little puppy feel. Pretty rotten.

As the little puppy continued her walk around the farm, she ran into the cow. "You must be new here," the cow said. "Well, little puppy, just remember: the farmer loves me more than any of the other animals. Do you know why? Because I give him milk. From this milk he makes butter and cheese. Since you don't give him any milk, you are of no use to him."

Well, you can imagine how this made the little puppy feel. More rotten than he already felt.

The little puppy continued her walk around the farm, and she ran into the sheep. "You must be new here," the sheep said. "Well, little puppy, just remember: the farmer loves me most of all. Do you know why? Because I give him wool to make warm clothes. Since you don't give him any wool, you are of no use to him."

Well, you can imagine how this made the puppy feel. Never in her short life had she felt so rotten.

The little puppy said, "The horse and the cow and the sheep are right. I don't pull any loads. I don't give any milk. I don't make any wool. I'm just a good-for-nothing puppy." And when she said that, big tears began to trickle down her cheeks.

That evening, when her master came home from working hard all day, the little puppy ran to meet him and play with him. After

Adapted from a fable by John Aikin, an English writer.

they had played a while, the master said, "You know what, little puppy? No matter how tired I am when I come home, you always make me feel happy. I wouldn't trade you for all the animals on the farm."

Now, my question is, Who is that puppy? And my answer is, You are. You make your mom and dad so happy and they love you so much that they wouldn't trade you for anybody in the whole world.

82

Lazy Bone

Once upon a time lived a little boy whose first name was Lazy. His last name was Bone. Lazy Bone.

Lazy Bone especially hated one thing. He hated learning hymns by heart. Whenever the boys and girls at his church were learning a new hymn, Lazy Bone would only pretend he was singing. What he actually did was sing a sentence he had thought up—a sentence that could be sung to all hymn tunes. The sentence was this: Racky sacky soo.

For example, when his class sang: "Silent night! Holy night! All is calm, all is bright," Lazy Bone would sing, "Racky sack soo! Racky sack soo! Racky sack, sacky soo." Or when his class would sing, "Onward Christian soldiers, marching as to war," Lazy Bone would sing, "Racky sacky soo-oo-oo, racky sacky soo."

Lazy Bone's mom and dad were very proud of him. They would say things like, "Isn't it amazing how many hymns our little boy knows? Why, there isn't one hymn he can't sing."

What they did not know, of course, was that Lazy Bone racky-sacky-sood every hymn.

This went on for many years so that by the time Lazy Bone

was seventy years old he still didn't know the words of a single hymn. Then one day he became very sick and hurt all over. At night he could not sleep and would lie awake for many hours. Lazy Bone thought, "If only I knew some hymns. Then I could sing them and the night wouldn't seem so long. It would also help me not to think about my pain."

But, of course, he didn't know any hymns. All he could sing was "Racky sacky soo."

I can hear you say, "That's just a silly story. A man by the name of Lazy Bone never lived. A man who racky-sacky-sood every hymn never lived." And you are right.

But I do know someone who, when he was very sick once and hurt all over, passed the long hours of the night singing hymns, one after the other.

I tell you one thing: he did not racky-sacky-soo any of those hymns. He didn't have to, because he started to learn them when he was your age.

83

Not Luck But God

Many years ago I lived in a country where a war was going on. During the last year of that war we had no electricity, no oil, no gas, no coal. The only thing that kept us warm was wood.

But where to get wood? Many trees were on our street, but nobody dared touch them. They were just too beautiful. Without them our street would look bare and ugly.

Still, we needed wood to stay warm and cook. So on a cold night in February, the people in our street decided to saw down all those beautiful trees.

Now, I should tell you that no one was allowed on the street after eight o'clock at night. If an enemy soldier caught you out on the street after that hour, you were in big trouble.

So here we all were, out on the street at a time when we were not allowed outside, sawing down trees. My dad, my brother, and I were attacking the tree in front of our house. I had climbed into the top of the tree to saw off the branches. From where I was, I could see the whole street. For snow lay on the ground and the moon was shining.

Suddenly I saw everybody disappear and run inside. When I looked down the street I saw why. Here, coming down our street, with a rifle slung over his shoulder, was an enemy soldier. He was riding on a bike.

It was too late for me to climb down and run inside. The only safe thing to do was to stay where I was and not move a muscle. Maybe the enemy soldier would not see me.

But how could he *not* see me? It was almost as bright as day and I had sawed off many of the branches. From the top of the tree I watched the soldier come closer and closer. Would he look up? Would he say, "You there up in the tree! Come down!"

You know what? The soldier never looked up. Was I lucky! That's what I told my mother as soon as I stepped into the house. "Boy," I said, "was I lucky!"

"What do you mean?" my mother said. "You weren't lucky at all. You were protected. For while you were out there, we were all watching you through the window and praying that God would make the soldier not see you. And God answered our prayer."

My mother was right. There is no such thing as luck. We escape danger, not because we are lucky, but because God protects us. And because we have parents who pray God to protect us.

84

Party Pooper Pig

Once upon a time lived a mother pig that had a son whose name was Squealer. She thought that Squealer was the most handsome little pig in town. She gave him a bath every day because she thought, "If I keep Squealer clean on the outside, everybody will like him."

One day the mail carrier brought a letter. It had Squealer's name on it. It read, "Dear Squealer, next Saturday at four o'clock in the afternoon we are having a birthday party. We invite you to come." It was signed "Dubby the Dog."

"Now, isn't that nice?" Squealer's mother said. "We must get you squeaky clean and put a curl in your tail."

You see, up until this time Squealer's tail had been as straight as a candlestick, and for a pig to look sharp the tail must be curly. Every pig knows that.

Adapted from Kenneth B. Welles, *Children's Sermons* (Philadelphia: Westminster) pp. 120–22. Copyright © 1954, 1982. By permission of Thomas Welles Barber.

When Squealer went to the party at four o'clock on Saturday afternoon, he was squeaky clean and curled.

Everything went fine until it was time for refreshments. Everything looked so good that Squealer couldn't help but make a pig of himself. He ate five helpings of cake. He drank ten glasses of Coke. And when ice cream was served, he had one bowl, then another and another and still another. Everybody stared at him. Never had they seen anybody eat so much so fast.

Finally someone said, "Squealer, you may be clean on the outside, but you're still a pig on the inside."

Jesus once said something like that. He said it to people who tried their best to look clean on the outside. He said to them, "It's not the outside that counts. What counts is the inside. What counts is your heart. If I don't live in your heart, sooner or later you are going to make a pig of yourself."

So every morning when you wash your face and comb your hair be sure to ask Jesus to make you clean inside. Otherwise . . . well, you know what. Otherwise sooner or later you're going to make a pig of yourself.

85

Toothpaste

Take a tube of toothpaste. Take off the cap and then gently squeeze it. Out comes a fat, shiny worm of toothpaste.

You do that each time you brush your teeth. But there's a problem. When you squeeze too hard, there's no way of putting the extra toothpaste back in.

Try it sometime. Try to put toothpaste back into the tube. That is impossible.

Words are like toothpaste. Once words leave your mouth, that's it. There they are. You can't put them back into your mouth again. That too is impossible.

Of course, it's better to waste toothpaste than it is to waste words. It's much better to make a mess with toothpaste than it is to make a mess with words. When you make a mess with toothpaste, you can clean it up before your mom or dad sees it. But how can you ever clean up the mess you make with words?

How can you clean up the mess when you say things like, "You're the stupidest person in the world!" or "I hate you!" or "Drop dead!"?

Once you say things like that, that's it! You can't put them back into your mouth again.

Of course, you can say you're sorry for having said them. That's the least you can do. But the damage has been done. The mess has been made.

You want my advice? Treat words the way you treat toothpaste. Don't squeeze the tube too hard!

Adapted from Dorothy Francis, *The Boy With the Blue Ears* (Nashville: Abingdon, 1979). Used by permission of Dorothy Francis.

86

Skyscrapers

In August 1952, I stood on the deck of a ship that was entering New York harbor. I had never been in New York before. This was to be my first time. So you can imagine how excited I was. I was especially excited about seeing the skyscrapers.

It was a big disappointment. As the ship approached the part of New York where the skyscrapers are, and as I got my first look at them, I thought to myself, "Is that all?"

Somehow, in my mind I had pictured them as much taller. After all, people called them skyscrapers—scrapers of the sky. But they weren't doing anything of the kind.

After I got off the ship, I took the subway to 34th Street. Now you probably don't know what's on 34th Street. The Empire State Building is. And in 1952 the Empire State Building was still the tallest building in the world.

Standing at the foot of the Empire State Building and looking straight up, I almost felt dizzy. "Wow!" I thought, "What height! This building is so high it must be scraping the sky!"

When I had looked at it from the ship, it hadn't looked very high. Now that I was standing at the foot of it, it looked very high.

The same is true of God. When you live far away from God, God doesn't seem great at all. Only when you stand at God's feet and look up, do you say, "How great you are!"

87

Seeing Upside Down

Once upon a time lived a little boy who was different from everybody else. This little boy walked upside down. He walked on his hands instead of on his feet.

As he walked upside down, he saw the world differently from the way everybody else did. He smelled the flowers without bending down. He saw the beauty of grass from close by. He saw the hundreds of insects who lived in the grass.

But his parents were very worried. They said, "He is a misfit. If he does not learn to walk on his feet like everybody else, nothing will become of him."

So they took him to a doctor. The doctor worked with him. She worked hard to make him walk downside up. It took a while, but gradually the little boy learned to walk like everybody else.

The parents were happy. The doctor was proud of her work. Now the little boy saw the world just like everybody else did. He no longer smelled the flowers without bending down. He no longer saw the beauty of the grass from close by. He no longer saw the hundreds of insects living in the grass.

Christians are like that little boy. They see things differently from everybody else. They see things upside down.

Many people don't like that. They say things like, "Christians are misfits" and "Christians do things the wrong way" and "Christians must see things like we see them."

I hope you never do. I hope you will always see things upside down. I hope you will always see things the way Jesus saw them.

Adapted from Robert Kysar, *John the Maverick Gospel.* Copyright © 1976 John Knox Press. Adapted and used by permission of Westminster/John Knox Press.

88

The Last Leaf

Some years ago I was raking leaves in our backyard. When I finished, I happened to look up. Guess what I saw? A single leaf. All the other leaves had dropped off. This was the only one left.

So I waited and waited. At last a strong wind blew across our yard and snapped off that last leaf. Down it came. And no sooner did it hit the ground than all the other trees clapped their hands and began dancing for joy. Things were getting wilder and wilder so that I finally shouted, "OK, that's enough! That's quite enough!"

But do you think they listened to me? Not at all. They kept on clapping and dancing. Then, after all the trees had calmed down, I asked, "Will one of you please tell me what this is all about?"

Then the biggest tree opened its mouth and said, "We know who you are. Your name is John Timmer. And you are a minister."

"That's correct," I said, "but what does that have to do with ruining my lawn?"

"You, a minister, don't know why we trees are so happy now that the last leaf has fallen to the ground?" the tree asked.

"I'm sorry," I said, "but I don't."

"Doesn't it say somewhere in the Bible," the tree asked me, "that after the last Christian has been born, God will make all things new?"

"Yes," I said, "something like that."

"Well," the tree said, "we trees are just as much looking forward to that as you Christians are. We are just as much waiting for God to make all things new as you Christians are. Therefore each year after the last leaf has dropped to the ground, we think of the last Christian whose birth we all look forward to,

A story combining Isaiah 55:12, Matthew 24:14, and fall chores.

and whose birth will mean the end of this old world and the beginning of the new world. And that makes us dance for joy."

When fall comes next time, watch for the last leaf to drop off a tree and drift into your backyard. Maybe you too will see the trees clap their hands and dance for joy. I said "maybe" because many trees don't know about the new world. Just as many people don't know about it.

89

The Wild Pigeon

Once upon a time, somewhere in a faraway wood, lived a wild pigeon. On a farm not too far from that wood lived some tame pigeons. The wild pigeon and one of the tame pigeons would often meet and talk.

One day they talked about food. The wild pigeon said, "I never worry about food. Every day I find enough food to eat. I've never known a day when I did not find food to eat. So why worry?"

"Why worry? Why worry?" one of the tame pigeons said. "If I were you I would worry a lot. What if one day you wouldn't find enough food to eat? What if you wouldn't find food for several days in a row? You would starve to death. Poor pigeon! How lucky we tame pigeons are. We don't have to worry about a thing. The farmer feeds us. And the farmer has enough food in his barn to feed us for the rest of our lives."

After the wild pigeon flew home that day he did some thinking. He thought, "It must be nice to know that enough food is stored up to feed you for the rest of your life. Here I am. I don't

Adapted from *Meditations From Kierkegaard*, trans. and ed. T. H. Croxall. Copyright © 1955 by W. L. Jenkins; renewed 1983. Adapted and used by permission of Westminster/John Knox Press.

even know whether there will be enough food for me tomorrow. Maybe I should store up some food. Then, when I don't find food some day, I can eat the food I stored away."

So early the next morning the wild pigeon began to store up food and hide it in secret places. But each time he went back to those secret places he found that some other animal had eaten it.

This made the wild pigeon look for better hiding places. But this made him so busy that he hardly had time to eat. Life was no fun anymore. All the wild pigeon did was hurry and worry, hurry and worry.

Finally, he couldn't take it anymore. "This is no way to live," he said. "I'm going to join the tame pigeons. That way I won't have to worry about food ever again." Then he flew off to the farm, moved in with the tame pigeons, and ate their food.

That same evening, when the farmer came by, he noticed the wild pigeon. He grabbed it, threw it in the air, and said, "Go back to where you came from. Wild pigeons don't belong on my farm."

Now, I have a question to ask. Who, do you think, is that wild pigeon? The answer is: You are! Jesus wants you to live as that wild pigeon did before that tame pigeon put worry into his head.

SPECIAL-DAY STORIES

90

An Angel Named James Murray

Once upon a time, up in heaven, lived a little angel. This angel was so little that other angels would often fly right past him and never see him.

None of the other angels knew where this little angel came from or what his name was. So they named him James Murray. Which is a rather unusual name for an angel. But, then, heaven is the kind of place where unusual things often happen.

All the angels loved James Murray. He was such a cheerful little soul. And he loved to make music. Of course, all angels do, but James Murray especially so. On his tiny flute he would play the tunes he heard other angels sing and the tunes he made up himself.

One day, right before Christmas, James Murray played a tune on his flute that was so beautiful all the angels stopped singing. "Who is playing that beautiful tune?" everyone asked. And soon it was whispered all around, "James Murray is!"

After James Murray finished playing, all the angels said, "But James! That was just beautiful! We've never heard this tune before. Where did you learn it?"

"Well," James Murray said, "I uh . . . I uh . . . I don't like to brag or anything, but I uh . . . I made it up myself. It's almost Christmas and I just felt, uh, inspired. That's all. No big deal."

Then the angels said, "James, you may be the littlest angel in heaven, but that tune is the greatest! We think everybody ought to learn it, everybody in heaven and everybody on earth."

And everybody has been learning it ever since. Well, almost everybody. For do you know which tune James Murray was playing that day? The tune of this song:

> *Away in a manger, no crib for a bed,*
> *The little Lord Jesus laid down his sweet head;*
> *The stars in the sky*

Looked down where he lay;
The little Lord Jesus asleep on the hay.

If you don't believe me, look it up in your hymnal or Christmas song book. When you look up the hymn "Away in a Manger," you will find that right below the words of the hymn it says, "Tune by James Murray." And James Murray is the little angel I've been telling you about.

91

Stable Talk

Let's pretend. Let's pretend we are in a stable where Jesus was born just a few hours ago. Let's pretend there is also a cow and a horse and a pig and a sheep. And let's pretend that the cow is saying to the horse, "Would you please stop sniffing in my ear. Ever since you woke up from your nap you've been sniffing. Why don't you blow your nose? Or better yet, why don't you cut off your nose? Your sniffing is driving me crazy."

The horse says, "Listen here, you dumb cow. You complain about me sniffing? What do you think you have been doing for the past hour? Nothing but chew, chew, chew. Nothing but drool, drool, drool. Your chewing and drooling are driving *me* crazy."

While the cow and the horse argue, the pig says to the sheep, "Do you have fleas or something? Ever since you got up this morning you've been rubbing your back against the stable wall. Why not ask the inn keeper to put some medicine on it?"

The sheep answers back, "Look who's talking! Mr. Pig himself! Do you realize, Mr. Pig, that you've been oinking ever since you finished eating your breakfast? I also think you need a bath and that you need it very badly. You not only *are* a pig, you also look like a pig."

As the animals argue back and forth, the stable door suddenly flies open and in walk some tough-looking characters. They're shepherds. One of them points to the baby Jesus and says, "There he is! There is the Savior the angel told us about!" Then they kneel down and worship baby Jesus.

The cow and the horse and the pig and the sheep can hardly believe their ears. Could that little baby over there be the Savior? But if the shepherds say so it must be true. So they too kneel down and worship baby Jesus.

Then, for the first time that day, all arguing stops. For when you kneel before Jesus and worship him, you don't feel like arguing any more, do you?

92

Opposite Land

Have you ever been in Opposite Land? Have you ever heard of it? If not, then let me tell you about it.

Opposite Land is a place where people do everything the opposite way. Where we live, people first are young and then grow old. In Opposite Land it's just the other way around. In Opposite Land people first are old and then grow young.

Where we live, people first breathe in before they breathe out. In Opposite Land it's just the other way around. In Opposite Land people first breathe out before they breathe in.

Where we live, children go to school during the day and sleep at night. In Opposite Land it's just the other way around. There children go to school at night and sleep during the day.

Where we live, people walk forward. In Opposite Land it's just the other way around. There people walk backward.

Now that you know what Opposite Land is like you are ready to listen to my story. It goes like this. Once upon a time there was a boy who lived in Opposite Land. His name was Tom. When it was Tom's birthday, he invited all his friends to his birthday party. They all brought presents. But because they lived in Opposite Land they did not give these presents to Tom, but exchanged presents with each other. Everybody got a present, everybody except Tom. He didn't get any.

This made Tom mad, real mad, so mad that he climbed on top of the piano and shouted, "Quiet everybody!" And when everybody was quiet Tom said, "You've all come to my birthday party. You've all brought a present. You've all received a present. I'm the only one who has not received a present. Whose birthday is it anyway? Yours or mine?"

That sounds a lot like the way most people celebrate Jesus' birthday, doesn't it? At Christmas these people exchange presents with each other. But what about Jesus? What present does he get? Whose birthday is it anyway?

93

What Shall We Give Him?

Imagine you lived in the days when Jesus was born. Imagine you were in the stable when Jesus was born. Imagine you understood animal talk. Then this is what you might have heard the rooster say: "What honor, what great honor, that Jesus was born in our stable!"

"You are so right!" the chicken said. "And to show you how thankful we are, why don't we each give Jesus a gift?"

"An excellent idea!" all the animals said. "But what can we give him, poor as we are?"

"Well," the chicken said, "I could give him one of my eggs."

"I wouldn't do that," the cow said. "Little babies don't eat eggs. All they do is drink milk. I'm going to give him some."

"I wouldn't do that!" the sheep said. "Babies don't drink cow milk. They drink their mother's milk. I think my gift is much better. I will give him my woolen coat for warmth."

"I wouldn't do that!" the donkey said to the sheep. "You know how freezing cold it gets here at night. If you give Jesus your woolen coat you'll freeze to death."

On and on the animals argued until, all of a sudden, the stable door flung open and in walked some tough-looking shepherds. As soon as they spotted baby Jesus, they knelt down and worshiped him. After a while they got up and left.

After they had gone, one of the animals said, "Did you notice that? None of the shepherds gave Jesus a gift. All of them received a gift from Jesus: Peace! You could tell from their faces. So peaceful! Jesus doesn't need our gifts. We need his gifts."

"You are so right!" the other animals said, and they all knelt down and worshiped baby Jesus. And as they did, they all received the gift of peace.

From that day on there was no more arguing in the stable. And that's why, to this day, stables are the most peaceful places in the world.

94

The Little Pine Tree

One of my favorite Christmas stories is that of a little pine tree in a far-away forest. This little pine tree thought, "Hey, what's going on here? Look at all those trees. They have leaves. Now look at me. I don't have any. I have needles. But I want leaves like everybody else."

So the little pine tree made a wish. It said, "I wish I had leaves." And because it was a proud little pine tree, it said, "I wish I had gold leaves." Because it thought, "This will make all the other trees jealous of me."

The next morning when it woke up the little pine tree had what it had wished for. Its branches were covered with leaves of pure gold. "Now I am more beautiful than all the trees in the forest," it said. "Look at me glitter! Look at me shine!"

But the same day a man with a large bag on his shoulders spotted the little pine tree. He stripped it of all its leaves, put them in his bag, and hurried home.

"I will never wish for leaves of gold again," the little pine tree said. "This time I wish for leaves of glass."

The next morning the little pine tree had what it had wished for. All its branches were covered with leaves of glass.

But that same day a strong wind began to blow so that all the glass leaves fell to the ground and broke into many pieces.

"I will never wish for glass leaves again," the little pine tree said. "This time I wish for green leaves—the same leaves all the other trees have."

The next morning the little pine tree had what it had wished for. Its branches were covered with green leaves.

But that same day a goat came by and ate all the leaves.

Adapted from Rose Dobbs, *Once Upon A Time: Twenty Cheerful Tales to Read and Tell.* Published and copyright © 1950 by Random House. Copyright © renewed 1977 by Rose Dobbs.

"Now I understand why God gave me needles instead of leaves," the little pine tree said. "Oh, how I wish I had my needles back again."

Well, you guessed it. The next morning the little pine tree's branches were covered with needles. And now, at last, the little tree was truly happy.

If, on Christmas Eve, you are unhappy with some of the gifts you received and wish you had received different ones, remember the story of the little pine tree. It may help you change your mind.

95

The Little Stranger

Once upon a time, in a deep, dark forest, lived a poor woodcutter. The woodcutter and his wife had two daughters whose names were Mary and Valentine.

One cold winter evening, as they were sitting around the fireplace, a knock came at the door. A voice cried, "Please, let me in. Please, let me in. I'm cold and hungry."

Mary and Valentine jumped up and opened the door. Standing outside was a little boy. "Come on in," they said. "Warm yourself near the fire. And here, have something to eat."

After the little stranger had eaten, Mary and Valentine said, "Why don't you sleep in our bed tonight? We'll sleep on the floor." And they did.

In the middle of the night, when everybody was sleeping, Mary suddenly woke up. "Did I hear music?" she wondered. "Listen! There it is again. Oh, what beautiful music!"

Quickly she woke up Valentine and together they rushed to

Adapted from a fairy tale of Hans Christian Andersen.

the window. And what do you think they saw? Standing in the snow was a group of children dressed in silver clothes, some playing golden flutes and others singing the most beautiful music.

As Mary and Valentine stood listening, they heard a noise behind them. They turned around and saw it was the little stranger. "I am the Christ Child," he said. "I wander through the world and knock on people's doors. Many people send me away. They say to me things like, 'Sorry, but we don't have room for you,' or 'Why don't you try next door?', or, 'We're too busy right now, too busy wrapping Christmas presents. Why don't you come back next month?' But you didn't do that. You took me in and gave me something to eat, and for that God will bless you."

As he said that, the little boy disappeared. But who knows at whose door he will knock next?

96

Ever Green

What do you do when the weather turns cold? You put on extra clothes. A sweater. A coat. A scarf. What do trees do when the weather turns cold? They do the opposite. They take off some of their clothes. They shed their leaves. Except one kind of tree. The evergreen tree keeps its leaves all year 'round.

Do you know why? An old Russian legend tells us why. Of course, it's only a story. It didn't really happen that way. But I thought you might like to hear it anyway.

This is how this story goes. When Jesus was born in Bethlehem, King Herod told his soldiers to kill all the baby boys in Bethlehem. Fortunately, they did not kill Jesus, because an angel had told Jesus' parents to escape to Egypt.

When King Herod heard about this he told his soldiers, "Go after them and kill their baby."

As Joseph and Mary hurried to escape from Herod, they came to a grove of trees. One of these trees was an evergreen. In those days people didn't call it an evergreen because, like all the other trees, it shed its leaves in the fall. Also, its branches did not hang down as they do today, but pointed upward.

As Mary and Joseph hurried past, something strange happened. The evergreen talked. It said, "Behind you I can see King Herod's soldiers coming. Quick! Hide under my branches."

Quickly Mary and Joseph ran to the tree. When they reached it, the tree let down its branches and covered them.

When King Herod's soldiers reached the tree, they rode right on past it. They never saw Mary and Joseph and the baby Jesus hiding under its branches.

When the soldiers were gone, God spoke from heaven. He said to the tree, "As a reward for saving Jesus' life, your branches will be green all year 'round. You will be ever green."

It's only a story, of course. But a beautiful one, isn't it?

97

Fastest Gun in the West

Once I watched a movie in which a tough-looking guy said, "I'm the fastest gun in the West!" Then his gun went BANG, BANG, BANG. And before the movie was half over he had hurt ten people.

But then another tough-looking guy came along and said to the first guy, "You are not the fastest gun in the West. I am!" Then his gun went Bang, and he shot the first guy.

When you fight others, others will fight you. When you hurt others, others will hurt you.

That's what Jesus told Peter in the Garden of Gethsemane. Soldiers had come to arrest Jesus. Peter wanted to defend Jesus, so he pulled out his sword. But Jesus said, "Leave your sword where it is, Peter. Don't pull it out. Don't fight with it. For all who fight with the sword will be hurt by the sword."

What Jesus told Peter reminds me of an old story. Once upon a time a mosquito looked at his stinger and said, "Isn't that a beauty? With this stinger I can even beat a lion."

Then the mosquito flew up to a lion and said, "Let's fight! Let's find out who is stronger, you or I." Then the mosquito began to sting the lion all over, on his nose, on his cheek, on his ear, on his leg, everywhere. The lion tried to swat the mosquito with his paw, but missed each time. At last the mosquito flew away, laughing. But while laughing he flew right into a spider's web.

As the spider came walking toward him to eat him, the mosquito thought to himself, "Isn't that strange? I beat a lion— the strongest animal in the world. But now I'm about to be eaten by a weak spider."

Jesus was right when he said to Peter, "People who fight with the sword will be hurt by the sword."

98

A Loose Tooth

Terrible things can happen to you when you are a child. One evening you go to bed with all your teeth firmly in place. The next morning you wake up and discover that when you press your tongue against your front teeth, one of them moves. And you think, "Oh oh! Something is definitely wrong!"

So you go to the bathroom, look in the mirror, press your tongue against your front teeth, and actually see one of them move. Again you think, "Oh oh! Something isn't quite right! Something is definitely wrong!"

Then you go downstairs and announce at the breakfast table, "Guess what? One of my front teeth is loose. Look!" And with your tongue you wiggle your front tooth back and forth, back and forth.

Then your older brother or sister says, "Let me pull it out for you. One quick pull will do it. You'll hardly feel it. It may bleed a little but that's all."

But you say, "Don't you dare touch my tooth! Don't anyone dare touch my tooth. It's my tooth and it's going to stay right where it has always been—in my mouth."

As days go by, things aren't getting any better. Your tooth becomes wigglier and wigglier. And the wigglier it gets, the harder it is to bite with it.

Does the Bible have anything to say about a loose tooth? Yes, it does. In Proverbs 25:19 it says that in time of trouble, you should not ask for help from someone who isn't reliable. To ask for help from an unreliable person in time of trouble is like biting into an apple with a loose tooth.

When Jesus was in the Garden of Gethsemane the night before he died, he asked Peter, James, and John to help him. He asked them to pray with him. But instead of praying with Jesus, they fell asleep. Jesus could not depend on Peter, James, and John. They were like three loose teeth in his mouth.

99

Banzai!

One of my favorite Easter stories is about a Japanese Christian whose first name was Kanzo and whose last name was Uchimura. Kanzo Uchimura. Do you think you can remember that name?

Before you can understand this story, you should know one thing. You should know that when Japanese people wish you good health and a long life, they shout, "Banzai!" The word *banzai* actually means ten thousand lives. So when you invite Japanese people to your birthday party and they shout, "Banzai!" they are actually shouting, "Ten thousand lives!"

Back to our story. Kanzo Uchimura suffered much during his life. He suffered when his wife died. He suffered when his second wife died. He suffered when his daughter Ruth died.

At the funeral of his daughter Ruth, when friends and family were standing around the grave, Uchimura spoke only a few words. This is what he said: "My daughter Ruth was old enough to get married. She was old enough to become a bride. But Jesus called her home to be *his* bride. Today is not Ruth's funeral. Today is her wedding."

The coffin with Ruth's body was lowered into the grave and each member of the family threw a handful of dirt on top of it.

When it was Uchimura's turn, he took a handful of dirt, raised it above his head, and shouted, "Banzai! Ruth is alive forevermore!"

Uchimura could shout that because he believed that on Easter Sunday Jesus became alive again, and that, when we die, we too will become alive again some day.

Today is Easter. What does Easter mean? Easter means that when someone who is a Christian dies, you can do what Uchimura did. You can stand at her grave and shout, "Banzai! Ten thousand lives! Life forevermore!"

100

Easter Hands

About one hundred years ago lived a famous painter named Renoir.

When Renoir grew old, his fingers and wrists became so stiff that painting became very difficult for him.

Did that keep Renoir's hands from painting? Not at all. One of his friends stuck the brush he needed between his stiff fingers and Renoir's hands went right on painting. Renoir's hands went right on blessing the world.

This story of Renoir's hands reminds me of the story of Jesus' hands. When Jesus lived on earth two thousand years ago, he used his hands to bless little children. He said, "Let the children come to me." There they came. Little Jonathan with his dirty face. Little Miriam with her runny nose. Little Mary with her scraped knee. Then Jesus put his hands on their little heads and said, "God bless you, Jonathan! God bless you, Miriam! God bless you, Mary!"

But then something terrible happened to Jesus' hands. People drove big, ugly nails through his hands. People nailed his hands to a piece of wood, so that his hands died.

Did that keep Jesus' hands from blessing little children? Not at all! For on Easter Sunday Jesus rose from the dead. On Easter Sunday Jesus' hands became alive again. On Easter Sunday Jesus' hands began blessing little children again.

That's what Easter is all about.

101

Dandelions

Most people don't like dandelions. They try to get rid of them. They put weed killer on them.

But I like dandelions. Do you know why? Because they remind me of Pentecost. Let me tell you why.

First, the flowers of dandelions are yellow. Then they turn into pretty white balls.

When you examine one of those pretty white balls you find that it is a ball of tiny parachutes. Hanging below each of these tiny parachutes is a tiny seed.

When the wind blows on these pretty white balls, it takes these tiny parachutes with their tiny seeds and scatters them all over your neighbors' yards, so that after a few weeks your neighbors also will have dandelions growing all over their lawns.

Dandelions go from few to many, and from many to millions. One dandelion makes ten other dandelions, and each of these ten new dandelions makes ten more dandelions, until there are millions of them and the whole world is covered with them.

This reminds me of Pentecost. On the day of Pentecost, almost two thousand years ago, Jesus' disciples were together in one place. Then God blew the wind of his Holy Spirit on them. Each of the disciples was like a tiny parachute with a tiny seed. God's wind blew them in many different directions. Some landed nearby, others far away. Some landed in their own country, some in other countries.

Wherever the disciples landed, they planted the tiny seed of the gospel. These tiny seeds grew and grew and became churches, until today there are almost as many churches as there are dandelions.

That's why I like dandelions. They remind me of Pentecost.

102

Memory

Each of us has a memory. Because we do, we remember things. You remember who your friends are. You remember what your name is. You remember who I am.

Now just for fun, let's pretend you do *not* have a memory. Let's pretend you do *not* remember things. Then what? Then you would do all kinds of crazy things.

For example, you would get up in the morning and ask, "Dad, do I brush my teeth with my comb? I don't remember." Or you would ask, "Mom, do I comb my hair with my toothbrush? I don't remember."

If you had no memory your dad would say to you at the breakfast table, "Don't pour milk over your sister! Pour it over your cereal! That's what milk is for, don't you remember?" Or your mom would say, "Don't put jam on your brother's hair, put it on your toast! That's what jam is for, don't you remember?" Or your brother would say, "Don't *eat* your napkin! Use it to wipe your sticky fingers! That's what napkins are for, don't you remember?"

And then you would say, "I'm sorry, but I forgot. I must have lost my memory."

In church too we need a memory, for in church we do a lot of remembering. For example, in church we remember that on the night before Jesus died, he ate a meal with his disciples. In church we remember that during that meal Jesus took a loaf of bread, broke it into pieces, and gave each of his disciples a piece, and said, "Take, eat, remember and believe that this is my body, which is broken for you."

Yes, in church we definitely need a memory. In fact, without a memory there would be no church. Without a memory there *could* be no church. Have you ever thought about that?